CHILDREN MATTER

BY

SCOTT PUGH

All Scripture quotations are taken from the Holy Bible, New International Version®, NIV®, Copyright © 1973, 1978, 1984 by International Bible Society.

To respect the privacy of the author's friends and students, most of the names in this book are pseudonyms. However, all events and other descriptions are factual to the author's best recollection.

ISBN: 978-1-4951-0553-1

Copyright © 2014

All rights reserved. No part of this book may be reproduced or transmitted in any form or by any mean, electronic or mechanical, including photocopying and recording, or by any information storage and retrieval system, without permission in writing from the author.

Cover designed by Jason Maric

Dedicated to my mom, Mary Pugh, for all the years you have made children matter. There aren't enough words to tell you how awesome I think you are. You have done more to impact the lives of young people than anyone I know. You're the best mom ever.

CONTENTS

Acknowledgements:		v
Foreword:		viii
Introduction:		1
Chapter 1:	Train	13
Chapter 2:	The James Syndrome	34
Chapter 3:	Actually You Can Send A Boy To Do A Man's Job	47
Chapter 4:	Put Your Money Where Your Mouth Is	59
Chapter 5:	Home Sweet Home	67
Chapter 6:	Now It's Personal	91
Chapter 7:	Partner With the City	99
Chapter 8:	Throw A Party	112
Chapter 9:	Slavery	135
Conclusion:		150

ACKNOWLEDGEMENTS

Vanessa, you have always called our relationship "fate" and I've never agreed with you, but I actually think you're right. There's no one else on planet earth who could (or would) put up with my crazy ideas, my zany impulses or my pace of life. I seriously think that you deserve some kind of major award for putting up with me. Thanks for being the best friend I've ever had, for making me laugh all the time and for being so supportive over the years. You really are the best wife and mom in the world. By the way, that samurai sword was sharp.

Owen, I really do think that you are smart, special and that you will be the best preacher in the world some day. I can't thank you enough for your laugh, your big personality or the way you pray for people. I've never seen anyone who has a bigger heart than you. By the way, we're camping out when it stops snowing in Cleveland – that means in August.

Madeline, you are truly a unique person. I'm not talking about your unbelievable personality. You are unique because *no one* has me wrapped around their finger more than you…yeah, it is ridiculous. Thanks for being so sweet and for letting me tell stories about you in this book.

Dad and Mom, you have been the biggest cheerleaders for everything I have ever wanted to do and you have supported every crazy decision I have ever made. Thanks for being the best parents ever and for all you do to serve at Velocity.

Larry and Ericka, thanks for all you have done to support our decision to start a church in Cleveland. There are hundreds of people who will be in heaven because of your love and support.

David Thorne, I've never had a better friend or co-worker than you. Thank you for going with me on this insane ride to reach people who are far from God and for giving your heart and soul to make this vision a reality. Velocity is a great church because of you…and I mean that more than you will ever know. We would never be where we are without you, Jessica and your kids.

Debbie Jones, thanks for your encouragement to write this. I didn't think that I would ever write a book. Then again, I didn't think I would ever move to Cleveland, plant a church, start Love Cleveland, be on the Children Matter team, etc., etc., etc. Seriously, you should be in sales. Can anyone tell you no?

Scott Baker, thanks for all you and Northwest Avenue Church did to help us start Velocity. We would never be where we are without you and your congregation.

Bridges Christian Church, Licking Valley Church of Christ, Southeast Christian Church, Northside Christian Church, Momentum Christian Church, I know I've told all of you this before, but thanks for supporting Velocity. None of these stories would have happened without you.

To all our friends and family at Velocity, we love you so much. Sharing our lives with you over the past five years has been more than a joy…it's been the best five years of our life. We are so thankful for you, your children and the way that God brought all of us together. We have a long way to go, but let's keep being a church that truly loves people far from God and let's keep making children matter.

Foreword

How This Book Came About

A few years ago, I went to a church planting meeting in Worthington, Ohio called Kingdom Synergy Partnerships (KSP). KSP is a collection of church leaders who get together to share ideas, resources and start new churches. KSP meets four times a year and each time we get together we have people who speak on different topics that relate to church planting, church growth and strategy.

When our staff showed up that morning, I had no idea what the topic of conversation was going to be. After some initial small talk with a few of the pastors, we sat down at a table and I found out that the topic of the day was going to be children. I was elated because children are my favorite people in the world. Put me in a room with 500 adults and students and I guarantee I will spend 90% of my time talking with the kids and teenagers in the room. It's not that I don't love adults, I do, but there's always been something very special to me about young people.

About 15 minutes into our morning session, a man stood up to give a presentation about a children's home for orphans. A few minutes into his talk, he said two words that literally turned my world upside down. I don't remember the subject or the predicate of his sentence, but in the middle of his sentence he spoke two words that sent my mind reeling. He said, "…children matter…" For some reason those two words hit me like a ton of bricks. It wasn't that I haven't heard someone say that before. I've heard those two words used a lot over the years, but this time was different. It was almost like a light came on for me. For the next three hours, I sat in my seat completely ignoring the rest of the presenters and I focused on those two words – *children matter*.

As I sat at the table, my mind raced at top speed. I started writing down all the verses of Scripture that I could think of that pertain to children. I thought about all the areas of life where Jesus told us to make children matter. I drew graphs, tables, and charts. Before I knew it, the program was over and it was time to leave.

When I got home that night, my mind wouldn't shut down. I tried to go to sleep but I couldn't. So,

I got up and went to my computer. I started to arrange all my random thoughts about children in an organized way. At three in the morning I stopped to read what I had been writing and my thoughts filtered down to four specific areas where Scripture clearly teaches that children matter. The four areas are:

- Children matter in our home.
- Children matter in our church.
- Children matter in our city.
- Children matter around the world.

Over the past two years, I have spent an enormous amount of time trying to help people, parents, pastors and church leaders understand how to make children matter in those four areas. As a result of that work, this book is a hands-on approach to make children matter in your home, church, city and around the world.

Introduction

I want to start off this book a little bit different. I want to start off by playing a game. Now before you roll your eyes, I need you to give me the benefit of the doubt for a second. You see, I was a youth minister for 14 years so I love games. Games are a great icebreaker and they allow you to get to know someone that you've never met before. This game is simple. All I want you to do is think about something that makes you angry.

BUT WAIT! Before you get started, I need you to know that this can be a very dangerous activity. So if you are reading this book while sitting beside your wife, this isn't the time to look at her and say, "You know what really makes me angry? I get so mad when your mom stops by the house unannounced." That wouldn't be the best decision.

If you're sitting beside your husband, this isn't the time to look at him and say, "I get really angry when you throw your clothes on the floor instead of putting them in the hamper."

If you're reading this book and your parents are in the same room, this isn't the time for you to pop off and say, "You know what ticks me off? I get really mad when you tell me I have to be home by 11 o'clock. My friends don't have to be home until midnight and that just isn't fair." Don't say that! If you do, you may be banished to your room for eternity.

So if this question is going to cause any disruption in your family, if it's going to cause any turmoil in your marriage, I need you to remember this is just a game. All I want you to do is take 10 seconds and think about something that makes you angry. Ready? GO.

I imagine it didn't take you very long to think of something that makes you completely irate because everybody has something that sets them off. All of us have our own personal boiling point. Not too long ago, I asked our staff and preaching team to tell me the things that make them angry. They said things like, "When you come to a stop light and there is a car in front of you, but when the light turns green, the car in front of you doesn't go." Someone else said, "I get angry when I go to the drive-thru and they don't get my order right and I have to go back." One of our female interns said, "I get so mad when people post stuff on Facebook that is no benefit to anyone."

We have an associate pastor at Velocity whose name is David Thorne and he's one of my best friends in the world. I've worked with Dave for over five years and he is the most easygoing, mild-mannered person I have ever met. To be honest in all our years working together, I've never seen David get mad about anything. So last week we were riding in my car and I asked him, "David, have you ever gotten really angry before?"

He answered (in his Clark Kent tone), "Yes. I've been angry before."

I said, "Really? Well tell me what set you off."

David said, "When I was in college, I walked into the bathroom and my roommate was using my toothbrush. So I looked at him and asked, 'Why are you using my toothbrush?' His roommate looked back at David and said, "Well Dave, in the three years we've been roommates, have you ever known me to own a toothbrush?" David discovered that for three years his roommate had been using his toothbrush every single day. Now I don't care who you are, that would not only make you want to vomit, it would make you very angry.

The truth is anger is an emotion that every person has to deal with at some point in their life. Even Jesus experienced moments of anger. One of the fascinating things about Jesus is that even though he is God's own son, Jesus had moments when he was extremely angry with people.

In fact, there are three specific times that we see Jesus get angry in Scripture. He got heated at the religious people of his day for their stubborn hearts and lack of compassion (Mark 3). He was so furious in the temple that he flipped over tables and drove out the moneychangers because they were nothing more than religious pickpockets (Matthew 21). We also see that Jesus got angry with his disciples because they neglected to remember how much children mattered to him.

> Mark 10:13 People were bringing little children to Jesus to have him touch them, but the disciples rebuked them. [14]When Jesus saw this, he was indignant.

The Bible tells us that one day as Jesus was traveling through the countryside people were bringing children to Him. They wanted Him to place His hands on them and bless them. They weren't asking for anything special. They just wanted Jesus to bless their kids. But when the disciples saw all these kids coming to Jesus, they rebuked them. The disciples were put off by the fact that these children wanted some of Jesus' time. The disciples had to be thinking, "Listen, Jesus doesn't have time for this. I mean there are people to heal and sermons to preach. Jesus doesn't have time to stop and care for all these children."

Jesus viewed the situation very differently. When he saw his disciples turning these children away, he was indignant. The word 'indignant' is a really nice, New Testament way of saying that Jesus was ticked off. The word indignant in the Greek language is the word *epitimao* and it means to find with fault, to censor severely or to charge sharply.[1] In other words, when Jesus saw his disciples pushing these children away, he got very angry with them and said:

> "Let the little children come to me, and do not hinder them, for the kingdom of God belongs to such as these. [15] I tell you the truth, anyone who will not receive the kingdom of God like a little child will never enter it." [16] And he took the children in his arms, put his hands on them and blessed them. Matthew 19:14

In Jesus' eyes, children weren't a nuisance and they weren't a waste of time. As a matter of fact, there isn't a group of people in Scripture that Jesus speaks more highly of than children.

> Matthew 18:1 At that time the disciples came to Jesus and asked, "Who is the greatest in the kingdom of heaven?"

So one day the disciples asked, "Okay Jesus, who is the greatest in the kingdom of heaven? Is Moses the greatest? Or what about Abraham, Isaac or Jacob? Who is the greatest person? What is the most important people group in the heavenly realms?"

To the disciples' amazement, Jesus did something very peculiar. He looked around this huge crowd of people and he called a little child to come and stand beside him. When Jesus called this child to stand with him, everyone in the audience had to be confused. They had to be thinking, "What does a little boy have to do with who is the greatest in the kingdom of heaven?" No one in this crowd of people listening to Jesus would have given this boy a second thought. After all, he was just a child, but Jesus didn't view children that way. Jesus thought that children mattered and that's why he said:

> "I tell you the truth, unless you change and become like little children, you will never enter the kingdom of heaven. [4]Therefore, whoever humbles himself like this child is the greatest in the kingdom of heaven." Matthew 18:3

Jesus used a different scale when he talked about how important children really are. Children weren't an afterthought; they were a group of people who truly mattered. He even called them the greatest in the kingdom of heaven. As the matter of fact, one of the most sobering realities that defines how important children were to Jesus is when he said:

> "And see to it that you do not look down on one of these little ones." Matthew 18:10

When Jesus said those 16 words, everyone in the audience must have gasped. Jesus' words must have shocked the crowd because no culture in history had ever given children equal footing to adults and certainly not the Romans in the first century. The Roman culture devalued children all together.

Paterfamilias

Ancient Rome was a man's world. Men held both the power and the purse strings. The head of the family was the oldest living male and he was called the "*paterfamilias*" which meant the "father of the family." The paterfamilias looked after the family's business, their property and could perform religious rites on behalf of the entire family. The paterfamilias had absolute rule over his household and his children, meaning that if his children made him angry, he had the legal right to disown them, sell them into slavery, or even kill them with no fear of being punished in any way. The paterfamilias even had the right to decide whether to keep a newborn baby.[2]

Back in Roman culture when a mother gave birth to a child, the midwife would place the newborn baby on the ground. If the paterfamilias picked the baby up off of the ground, it was formally accepted into the family. But, if he didn't pick up the child, if the decision went the other way, the baby was taken outside and abandoned. So if a child were born with some kind of handicap or if the paterfamilias didn't think that the family could support another child, the infant would be taken outside and completely abandoned. It is assumed that an abandoned child would be picked up and raised as a slave. That's how children were treated in the first century.[3]

So when Jesus said, "Don't you even look down on these little ones," that must have sent shockwaves to the ears of his listeners because they knew how children were treated. Children weren't treated as people, but as commodities that could simply be disposed.

Do you know why Jesus was so passionate when he spoke about the importance of children? Do you know why he was so angry with his disciples for keeping the young people away from him? The answer is really simple. It's because children mattered to Jesus….and they should matter to us.

That's what this book is about. It's about making children matter. Throughout the next several chapters, I will give you practical ways to make children matter in your home, in your church, in your city and around the world. By the way, this book isn't a theological hodgepodge of random Bible verses about kids. This book isn't about choosing the right curriculum for your children's program. This is a hands-on, let's get to it, there-is-no-tomorrow approach to making children matter....and it's time. It's time for people like you and it's time for people like me to take the words of Jesus seriously when it comes to children. It's time for us, as followers of Jesus, to start going to the extremes to make a huge difference in the lives of young people. Why? Because if we would begin to view children the way that Jesus viewed children, the world would forever be changed.

---

1. Epitimao (Def. 5). In NAS New Testament Greek Lexicon, Retrieved January 1, 2014, from http://www.biblestudytools.com/lexicons/greek/nas/epitimao.html.

2. PBS. The Roman Empire in the First Century: Family Life. Retrieved November 30, 2013, from http://www.pbs.org/empires/romans/empire/family.html

3. PBS. The Roman Empire in the First Century: Family Life. Retrieved November 30, 2013, from http://www.pbs.org/empires/romans/empire/family.html

Section I: Home

Two weeks ago, I took my daughter Madeline on a date. It's not unusual for us to do that because we go on dates pretty often. They're a great way to spend some quality time together – just the two of us. This particular date was special because I was taking her roller-skating, which is her favorite thing to do.

As we were driving to the rink, Maddie began to tell me why she wants to be a pediatrician when she grows up. She also told me how many children she wants to have. As I listened to her talk about having children, my first reaction was, "They better be adopted children because there's no way you're getting married." Of course, I didn't say that to her, I just listened.

As we drove down the highway, Madeline asked me what I thought about her plans. I said, "Maddie as long as you live the life that God has called you to live, Daddy will be happy. I will be happy if you choose to be a doctor or a ditch digger, as long as you understand how much God loves you."

A few minutes later, we pulled into the parking lot and we spent the next two hours skating in circles together. We laughed, danced along to the music, and when it was time to leave, she gave me a big hug and said, "Thank you so much daddy. I had the best time."

Driving home that night, I was reminded that there is no bigger privilege than to be a parent. It's one of the highest honors that God could bestow because he is giving a parent the opportunity to raise another human being to understand how much He loves them. This is such an important subject that the pages of Scripture are filled with verses that instruct, encourage, and challenge parents "to train a child in the way he should go."

Why did God give so much instruction about the importance of parenting? Because the children in your home are the greatest gift that God could give you and they really do matter. God has given you the responsibility to train them in such a way that they end up not only educated, well-adjusted adults, but that they are truly followers of Jesus.

Throughout this first section, I will share two practical ways that you can make YOUR children matter. These steps aren't complex, but they are critical if you really want your children to grow up to know and understand the reality of God's love.

CHAPTER 1

Train

One of my favorite things to do is run long distance races. I don't think there's anything more enjoyable than to run a half-marathon, marathon, or to finish a triathlon. There's no better feeling than to cross the finish line in a race like that, but there's nothing easy about training for a race like that either. That kind of training is hard! It requires me to get up 5 a.m. every day, lace up my shoes, and run 40-70 miles a week. I have to cross train by swimming, biking, and doing core exercises. I have to eat right, understand how my body feels to avoid injury, and prepare myself mentally for the physical beating I'm going to put myself through on race day. But if you put in the time and the miles, then more than likely you will be able to cross the finish line with ease.

Well, let's just say that you wake up one day and decide that you want to run a marathon, a 26.2 mile race. However, instead of doing the training yourself, you come to me and say, "Scott, I have the goal of finishing a marathon, but I want you to train for me. I want you to run 6 days a week. I want you to eat right, do wind sprints, and get eight hours of sleep every night. I want you to train like crazy, so that when race day comes, I'll be ready."

That wouldn't make any sense at all. If I trained for you, if I did the runs, if I did the cross trains, if I got plenty of sleep, then the only person who would be ready on race day is me. It wouldn't make sense to delegate the responsibility of your training to someone else if you wanted to complete the task. The odd thing is that many parents have been doing that for years when it comes to training their children. Let me explain what I'm talking about.

According to Scripture, parents are responsible for training and discipling their children. Parents are the ones who will be held accountable for the Biblical principles that they have instilled in their children. But for some reason, many parents have transferred that training responsibility to the church. Some parents think that if they take their kids to church every Sunday and drop them off in the children's area, the church will give their children all the spiritual training that they need to prepare them for all of life's challenges. They honestly believe that as long as they take their kids to church and expose them to spiritual teaching, they have fulfilled their responsibility because the church will do the training for them.

The problem is… that thought process is not in the Bible. Nowhere in Scripture are parents instructed to transfer the responsibility of discipling their children to the church. In fact, the Bible teaches just the opposite. Scripture clearly indicates that parents are responsible for training their children to understand what it means to follow Jesus. Consider the following examples:

> Ephesians 6:4 Fathers, do not exasperate your children; instead, bring them up in the training and instruction of the Lord.

> Colossians 3:21 Fathers, do not embitter your children, or they will become discouraged.

> Proverbs 22:6 Train a child in the way he should go, and when he is old he will not turn from it.

> Hebrews 12:10 Our fathers disciplined us for a little while as they thought best; but God disciplines us for our good, that we may share in his holiness. [11]No discipline seems pleasant at the time, but painful. Later on, however, it produces a harvest of righteousness and peace for those who have been trained by it.

Deuteronomy 11:18 Fix these words of mine in your hearts and minds; tie them as symbols on your hands and bind them on your foreheads. [19]Teach them to your children, talking about them when you sit at home and when you walk along the road, when you lie down and when you get up. [20]Write them on the doorframes of your houses and on your gates, [21]so that your days and the days of your children may be many in the land that the LORD swore to give your forefathers, as many as the days that the heavens are above the earth.

According to the Bible, a parent's number one responsibility is to train their children to understand the truth of Scripture and the reality of God's love. That's not the churches responsibility. That's the parent's responsibility! The church is supposed to come alongside what's already happening at home. As a parent, you have the responsibility to teach your children about God's redeeming love for mankind and that's not a once-in-a-lifetime conversation. That's an ongoing process because parents are instructed to train their children when you sit with them at home, when you drive down the road, when you lie down, and when you get up.

Read With Them

The great part about discipling your children is that there are so many methods that parents can choose to teach their children about God's love. One of the best and easiest ways is to read the Bible with your children. Simply boxing out a few minutes every day to read the Scripture together makes a world of difference. You don't have to read for an hour. It doesn't have to be some long, drawn out exegetical Bible study on the horses of Revelation. Just take a few minutes to read the Bible with your children every day.

Before we go on, can I say something to those of you who are new to following Jesus? I've worked with a lot of people just like you and I'm so happy you have given your life to Christ. But one of the things that many people in your situation tell me is that they feel very uncomfortable reading the Bible with their kids because the Scripture doesn't make sense. As a matter of fact, I can't tell you how many new believers have said to me, "Scott, I don't want to read the Bible with my kids because it doesn't even make sense to me yet. What if they ask me a question I can't answer?"

If you are in that situation, let me give you a really easy way to alleviate the pressure that you feel. Go to your local bookstore and find a good children's Bible to read together. Just start off by reading a kids Bible. Not only will that teach your children more about Jesus, it will help you understand the basics of Scripture as well. If your child is just learning to read, have them read out loud and ask them to explain what the story meant to them. Don't be intimidated by how much you do or don't know about the Bible, just be committed to reading with them every day.

Play Games

Another thing you can do to add some variety to your reading time is to play games. Why? Because kids love games and it keeps them engaged in the learning process. One of the games that Vanessa and I play with our kids to spice up our "training sessions" is an activity called *One Minute Sermon*. The way the game works is we read a story with our kids in their children's Bible, then one at a time, we have them stand up and give a "one minute sermon" on the story that we just read. We ask them to repeat the story that they just heard in their own words and then tell us why that story is important. They only have one minute to tell the story and we actually time it with a stopwatch. Our kids go crazy over this game.

A few weeks ago, we were reading the story of how Joseph in the Old Testament was sold into slavery by his brothers and then sent to prison for a crime he didn't commit. After we read that story, my daughter Madeline got up to do her one-minute sermon. She gave a quick recap of the story and then she went on to tell us why it was important. Madeline said, "You know, no matter where Joseph was, God was still with him. When he was in that pit, God was with him. When Joseph was sold as a slave, God was with him. When he was put in prison, God was with him. I think that story is important because no matter what happens in life, whether it's good or bad, God is still with me. I just need to trust him, even though I don't know where he's at." I may be a little biased, but I think that was the best sermon I've ever heard. It was short, to the point, and it actually made sense.

The Box

Mike and Olena Moores, a couple from our church, did a really fun activity with their girls during their devotion time one Advent season. They wanted to teach their kids about the 400 years of silence that took place between the Old and New Testament, but were unsure how to go about it. A few days later, they came up with a great idea.

One night in early December, they took an Advent calendar that their girls loved and put it in a box. Then they called the girls into the room and made them two promises. First, they promised the girls that they would love what was in the box. The second promise they made was that they would get to open the box. They didn't tell them when they would get to open it, just that they would.

The next step was they had the girls go and sit in front of the box in their living room. Olena gave her kids the following instruction, "Don't get up. Don't open the box. Just sit in front of it." Then without the girls seeing, she set a timer for five minutes. After that, she and Mike sat down on the couch and they did not talk to each other, or their kids, for five minutes. They just sat in total silence. Her kids had no idea what to think and they alternated from being excited to being worried.

"Mom? Are we in trouble? Do we still get to open the box? What did we do wrong? Why won't you answer us?"

Then the girls switched from nervousness to boredom, to humming, to snapping their fingers, to anger, and then dissatisfaction. After five minutes, Mike and Olena broke the silence and asked the girls how they felt about waiting so long without hearing anything from them. Then they went on to teach the girls the lesson that they wanted them to understand. They told them that God was silent for 400 years, but before God was silent, he made a promise to the Israelites that He would send a Savior who would be born in Bethlehem. But after

400 years of not hearing from God, maybe they thought God abandoned them. Maybe they thought God was mad at them. Maybe he forgot about them. Then they shared how the birth of Jesus was God keeping his promise that he made a long time ago. They had a very lengthy discussion and the girls were totally engaged and excited the whole time.

There's No Hurry

The truth is there are all kinds of books, curriculum, games, and activities that you can use to teach your children what it means to follow Jesus. But one of the most important things to remember when you are training your children is to take your time. Don't rush through a story in the Bible as fast as possible so that you can get finished, kiss them goodnight, and race down the stairs to spend time on Facebook or watch another episode of your favorite TV show. Make this the most important time of your day.

The other day, my son Owen and I were lying on his bed talking before bedtime. He was telling me what some of the students in his class were doing to be funny. As he was telling me this story, I didn't think what his classmates were doing was funny at all. I didn't get mad at him for telling me this story, I just listened. If I would have gotten angry that would have shut down our lines of communication and he would have clammed up immediately.

As I sat there listening to him, I started thinking about what I should say in reply. When he finished telling me his story, I grabbed my Bible off the shelf and read Owen the story about Hophni and Phineas. They were two young guys whose behavior wasn't what it should have been. They were called to be leaders among God's people, but they weren't acting like leaders. I read him the story and then I said, "Now Owen, tell me what you think about how those two boys acted."

He said, "They didn't do the right thing, Dad."

I said, "That's right! They didn't do the right thing and their actions caused a lot of people harm because they weren't being the kind of leaders that God expected them to be." Then I said, "Owen, there's something I want you to remember for the rest of your life. Leaders are people who set an example for everyone else to follow. So when you see people doing things you know they shouldn't do, you need to be different. In moments like that, you need to be a leader and set the kind of example you want everyone else to follow."

We talked for several more minutes about what it means to be a leader and setting a good example. He asked me a bunch of questions about leadership. Then we wrapped up our time by praying for the Compassion International kids that we sponsor, his classmates, our family and for God to develop him into the leader he's been called to be. It was a great learning and sharing time for us.

Moments like that will only happen if you choose to take the time to train your children. When Owen told me that story, if I had been half-heartedly listening because I was more interested in what was on television or reading what my friends are posting on Facebook, then that teachable moment would have never happened and I would have been doing a disservice to my son. As a parent, you need to take the responsibility of training your children seriously.

Triathlon Training

I really never understood the concept of serious training until I met Corey Fidler. Corey is a good friend of mine who is a podiatrist. But he isn't just a foot and ankle specialist, he is also one of the best athletes I have ever met. Corey is an awesome soccer player, baseball player and he's so good at football that he was the starting tailback for his college football team. No matter what sport Corey plays, he's one of those rare individuals who just excels. He's such a good athlete that he has completed two ironman triathlons, which is no easy task. An ironman is a race where you swim 2.4 miles, bike 112 miles and run a marathon – in the same day! Yeah, he's kinda insane.

About three years ago, Corey challenged me to train for a triathlon. I told him that I wasn't really interested because I didn't have some of the equipment that I needed, including a bike. To be honest, the real reason I wasn't interested is because it sounded really hard. Of course, I didn't tell him that. It was much easier for me to use equipment as an excuse.

After hearing my initial reasons, Corey told me not to worry because he would give me all the training gear that I would need. A few days later, he showed up at my house with a trunk full of gear. He gave me shorts, shirts, pants, gloves, two different helmets, and he even loaned me a bike to ride. He unloaded all of this stuff out of his car and put it in my garage. Then he handed me a training schedule and told me to get started.

Since I was out of excuses, I decided that I would at least give it a try. I knew that I could do the run. I love to run and I've raced that distance before. What I hadn't done before is swim or bike. Sure I've swum a few laps in a pool and I rode a bike when I was a kid. But this wasn't going to be a 2-lap swim or simply riding my bike down to the stop sign and back like I did when I was young. This was a long race.

I started training the very next day. I took the running part of my training very seriously and averaged a minimum of 40 miles a week. But when it came to the bike and the swim portion of the training, well let's just say I didn't take those so serious. Every two or three days, I would hop on the bike Corey loaned me and I would ride 5 or 6 miles. I would go to the pool and swim for 10 minutes every now and then, but I definitely didn't put the same amount of time and intensity into those areas as I did the run portion of the race.

After three months of training, Corey told me that I should do a "test run" to see how my overall fitness was developing. So I signed up for a sprint triathlon because those distances are much shorter. It's only a ½ mile swim, a 26-mile bike and a 3.1-mile run. I thought I could do a race like that with no problem….at least that's what I thought.

On the day of the race, I got up early and drove to the race site. I got my gear in place, headed to starting line, got into the water, and anxiously waited for the gun to go off. When the race began, I started swimming like crazy. I paddled as fast as I could, but about halfway through the swim I was dying. I floundered and flopped around the water like a dying fish.

After what seemed like an eternity, I finally got to shore and headed to my first transition, which was the bike portion of the race. I ran up the hill, threw my shoes on, jumped on the bike and started peddling. I was already a little tired because of the swim, but I just kept going. About 22 miles into the bike ride, I wasn't just a fatigued, I was whipped.

As I approached the last transition of the race, I set my bike on the rack, changed my shoes, and started running the 3.1 mile portion of the race. I knew that I was tired, but I also knew that running was the part of the race that I was most confident. After all, I've run much longer distances. I even ran cross-country and track in high school. What I didn't anticipate is how I would feel after the other two events. This was, without a doubt, the longest 5k of my life. I felt like I was carrying someone on my back the entire time. When I crossed the finish line, I could not believe how hard that race was. I thought it was going to be easy, but I was wrong.

On my way home, I called Corey to tell him how the race went. I told him about how I struggled on the swim, how the bike was really difficult and that the run seemed like an eternity. Being the straight shooter that he is Corey said, "Scott, there are two ways to train for a triathlon. The right way…and the way you are doing it. If you really want to finish a full triathlon, then you have to take it seriously. So you need to take your training seriously or don't train at all."

To be honest, that's not what I wanted to hear. I wanted Corey to say, "You did great for your first race. The goal is just to finish. Good job man." He definitely didn't say that, and as much as I didn't want to hear it, Corey was right. If I was going to train to finish an Ironman, I had to take it seriously.

The same is true when it comes to training your children. If you are going to disciple your children to follow Jesus, then you have to take it seriously. It can't be a once-a-month activity. You can't train them when you feel like it. You can't pray with them once a week and expect to get amazing results. You can't expose them to the poor one hour a year and think that they will develop a compassionate heart for people in poverty. You have to train them on a consistent basis.

You see, God wants us to disciple our children to be loving, joy-filled, patient, kind, good, faithful, gentle and self-controlled. But there's nothing easy about training your children to exude the fruit of the spirit. They aren't born spiritual champions. They have to be trained. Children must learn how to live out their faith in Jesus, and most of the time they will learn how to follow Jesus by emulating their parents. Consider the following example:

> II Timothy 1:5 I have been reminded of your sincere faith, which first lived in your grandmother Lois and in your mother Eunice and, I am persuaded, now lives in you also.

The Apostle Paul wrote this verse of Scripture to a young pastor whose name was Timothy. In this passage, Paul brings to the surface a very poignant reality about how children learn to follow Jesus. He indicates that Timothy got his faith from his grandmother Lois and his mother Eunice. As a matter of fact, Paul even uses the phrase "sincere faith" to describe how seriously these two women took following Jesus. They didn't just verbalize their faith in God - they actually lived it. These ladies took their training seriously, and as a result, Timothy had become quite a man of God.

Parents shouldn't fool themselves to think that their children aren't perceptive. They are! Kids are smart and they can tell over a period of time whether a parents' faith is real or not. They see how their parents handle pressure, what makes them upset, how honest they are on the telephone, what they think is funny, and what their priorities really are. No matter how much parents talk about following Jesus, it won't mean very much unless there is a consistent lifestyle that reinforces what they say they believe. When young people see their parents living out what it really means to follow Jesus, the chances of them growing into the people God created them to be increases greatly. The opposite is true as well. If parents don't take their faith seriously, if they don't teach their children what it means to follow Jesus, the results can be devastating.

One Generation

Do you remember back in the book of Exodus when God led the nation of Israel out of slavery in Egypt? God rescued the Hebrew people from Pharaoh, he helped them cross the Red Sea, he provided them with manna, and eventually, they entered the Promised Land. However, when the Israelites came to the Promised Land, God told the Hebrew people to make sure that they educate their children on all that He had done for them.

But for some reason, those parents never took God's instruction seriously. They didn't tell their children about all that God had done for them. They didn't teach them to follow God wholeheartedly. Eventually all those parents died and that generation grew up as a group of people who never understood how God expected them to live. And here's how the Bible describes that generation of people.

> Judges 2:10 After that whole generation had been gathered to their fathers, another generation grew up, who knew neither the

LORD nor what he had done for Israel. ¹¹Then the Israelites did evil in the eyes of the LORD and served the Baals. ¹²They forsook the LORD, the God of their fathers, who had brought them out of Egypt. They followed and worshiped various gods of the peoples around them. They provoked the LORD to anger ¹³because they forsook him and served Baal and the Ashtoreths. ¹⁴In his anger against Israel the LORD handed them over to raiders who plundered them. He sold them to their enemies all around, whom they were no longer able to resist. ¹⁵Whenever Israel went out to fight, the hand of the LORD was against them to defeat them, just as he had sworn to them. They were in great distress.

The Bible says that it took one generation, just one generation of parents who didn't pass the baton of faith on to their children for everything to go haywire, and the result was that their children were in great distress. The children in our society are no different. We have a generation of young people who are in great distress, and I honestly believe that one of the reasons so many students are struggling is because they have never been taught that obedience to God brings wonderful blessing and disobedience brings harm. Those truths are woven through the pages of Scripture.

As surely as you teach your kids their primary colors and their ABC's, take the time to teach them about God's redeeming love for all mankind. Make the time to disciple your children and take that training seriously. Don't pawn that responsibility off on the church. Don't think that your child's one hour at church on Sunday morning is the answer because it isn't. Training your children is your responsibility and most of the time they will emulate what they see in their parents.

Section II: Church

Pastoral Advisory

Let me start off Section II of this book by telling you two important things. First, this book is about making children matter. It's about pouring your time, your energy, and your love into a generation of people who are starving for attention and affection. Nothing in this section is theoretical. It's a straight-up approach that I have used for the past 20 years to make children matter in a church setting and it works.

Second, if you are trying to use children as leverage to get more adults to show up at your Sunday morning worship service, go ahead and skip this entire section. Just turn to Section III and keep reading. The reason I tell you that is because for far too long children have been used as a pawn in very sick and twisted church growth strategy which we will discuss in the chapter called *Put Your Money Where Your Mouth Is*.

Section II of this book will separate the men from the boys, the women from the girls, and the churches who truly care about kids from those who don't. So if you are looking for methods to impact the young people who are a part of your church in real ways, then read on. If you are looking for some quick church growth strategy that is leveraged on the backs of children, go ahead and skip to Section III.

CHAPTER 2

The James Syndrome

There are some passages of Scripture in the Bible that are nothing short of brutal. They are convicting. They are challenging. They make you think about your life in completely different ways.

Such is the case with the entire book of James. Any time I start feeling good about myself, all I have to do is open my Bible and start reading the book of James. There is one particular section of James that has always been very convicting to me over the years. The verses are found in James chapter two and talk about showing favoritism.

> James 2:1 My brothers, as believers in our glorious Lord Jesus Christ, don't show favoritism. ²Suppose a man comes into your meeting wearing a gold ring and fine clothes, and a poor man in shabby clothes also comes in. ³If you show special attention to the man wearing fine clothes and say, "Here's a good

> seat for you," but say to the poor man, "You stand there" or "Sit on the floor by my feet," [4]have you not discriminated among yourselves and become judges with evil thoughts?

I would imagine that most followers of Christ would never give a poor person a bad seat in the worship center because they weren't dressed like the guy on the cover of GQ. Nor could I picture the moment when someone's financial status would determine whether they sat in the front or back row.

However, I have seen a form of favoritism happening to children for years. Let me explain. Many times when people walk in the doors of our churches on Sunday morning, the adults (greeters, pastors, etc.) will say hello to the other "grown-ups." They will greet them with handshakes and hugs. They will ask questions about their week, their work, and they will even talk about the NFL season.

But far too often, the children who are standing beside these adults get overlooked. People don't ask them about their week, their band concert or their Little League game. They basically ignore them. I'm not sure if it's intentional, but sometimes I wonder if it is. After all, you have to greet adults because "grown-ups" are important.

They are the ones we want to fill the pews so they can hear the pastor's amazing oratory skill. Adults are the ones throwing big bucks in the offering plates to pay the bills, but when kids walk in the door, it's almost like they are invisible. Many of them aren't greeted with hugs and high-fives. Most of the time we rush them back to a youth room where a rag tag band of frazzled volunteers do their best to teach them about God's love.

Just as you come in on Sunday morning and want someone to acknowledge you, shake your hand, and ask how you are doing, the young people in our churches want the very same thing. They want to know that someone at that church, other than their parents, really loves and cares about them. Even if you aren't a child fanatic like me, I think there are several specific things we can do to let students know how important they are when they walk in the doors of our church.

First, be friendly and say hello to them. When you see a young person in the hallway, stop and say hi to them. Ask them how they're doing. Ask them if they are playing any sports. Ask how things are going at school. Just take a few seconds and show them that they really matter. I know this may sound overly simplistic, but I can't even begin to tell you how important that is, especially with teenagers. The reason I bring up teenagers is that

I've noticed the older many adults get, the more uncomfortable they feel around teenagers.

Who's Afraid of the Big Bad Wolf?

Several years ago, when I would recruit adult volunteers for our youth ministry, I would meet with every new prospect before they came to our program and here's what I would tell them. I would say, "Now listen to me. You are going to feel very out of place for a few weeks until you get to know some of the students because there are going to be over a hundred of them and only fifteen adults. So don't be a wallflower. Don't stand in the corner waiting for the students to talk to you. You take the lead and talk to them. Believe me, they are much more afraid of you than you are of them. Don't be afraid of the Big Bad Wolf."

No matter how much coaching I gave them, the same thing happened every time. The first week a new volunteer would come into the youth room, I would see him or her standing in the corner by themselves, scared to death of all the high school students. So I would walk over to them and say, "Now remember, don't be a social nomad. Meet students as soon as possible. I can tell by the look on your face that you are feeling really awkward." Some of these new volunteers would be completely freaked out and they would say, "But

Scott, look at them. I mean that guy has black hair and black clothes and black fingernail polish. He looks so scary."

Then I would say, "Now wait a minute. Let me tell you how he got to look that way. He got in his parents car, drove to the mall and walked into Hot Topic®. He bought those pants, that shirt and his studded belt buckle for $60. Then he went to Wal-Mart® and got hair dye and black fingernail polish. After that, he went home, dyed his hair, painted his nails, put on his new clothes, and came here. That means if you had $60, you could look just like that. Don't be afraid of them. Just go over and say hello."

Eventually they would muster up enough courage to walk over and talk to them. Within just a few weeks, those volunteers fell in love with the students and couldn't wait to see them every week. Even if you feel like you don't understand the teenagers in our culture. Even if they look different, talk different, dress different, make an effort to greet them and make them feel important on Sunday morning.

Kids Are People Too

That principle doesn't just apply to teenagers, it applies to young children as well. Several months ago, a little 4th grade girl named Miley walked into our church one Sunday morning. I was sitting on a bench talking with a group of adults and Miley looked in my direction, but she walked by me without saying anything, which is a total no-no at Velocity.

You see, the kids from our church know that I only have one rule. I don't have many rules, but I do have one. My rule is that no student (child or teenager) is allowed to come into Velocity and not say hi to me. That's my one and only rule. I stand at the door every Sunday with the sole purpose of saying hi to as many students as I can because I want them to know that they are special to me.

So Miley walked into the building, glanced in my direction and kept on walking. Even though I was surrounded by adults, I dismissed myself from the conversation, called her name, and waved at her to come back and talk to me. She walked through the crowd of guys who were talking about Ohio State football and sat down beside me on the bench.

After Miley sat down, I asked her how school was going. She said, "Scott, it's not going well. There are some boys in my class who make fun of me because they say that I have big feet and it really hurts my feelings."

As I sat there listening to Miley tell me about how her feelings were hurt, the "dad" part of me wanted to drive to her school and set those boys straight. I knew I couldn't do that. So I started thinking about what I could say to her. A few moments later I said, "You know Miley, there were some people in the Bible who said some really horrible things about Jesus."

"They did?"

"Yes they did. They said all kinds of unfair things about Jesus. They called him names, they made fun of him, and they did even worse things than that. But you know what? Jesus did some really great things even though people were mean to him and I think that you are going to do some really great things with your life too. Don't let what those boys said to you keep you from being the person that God created you to be. I think that you are really super special."

Miley got a big smile on her face and said, "Thanks Scott." Then she gave me a hug and went on her way. I have no idea what my sermon was about that day because I don't remember. I don't remember the title, the text, or the sermon series. But I will never forget the conversation that I got to have with Miley that morning because that was a moment when I got to make a child matter.

Those conversations are quite possible in your church too. Not only are they possible – they are necessary. Don't believe me? I will prove it to you.

In the spaces below, I want you to write the names of the five most influential sermons that you've ever heard. I want you to include the pastor who preached it, the date the message was delivered, the text they used, and how it impacted your life. Ready? GO.

Title of sermon   Date   Verse(s) Used   Impact
1. _____   ____   _____   _____
2. _____   ____   _____   _____
3. _____   ____   _____   _____
4. _____   ____   _____   _____
5. _____   ____   _____   _____

I would imagine that some of you could probably recall two or maybe three sermons that impacted your life.

Next, write down the names of 5 people who made you feel special growing up. It could be a teacher, coach, parent, grandparent, friend, neighbor, etc. Take a minute and write them down.

Adults Who Made You Feel Special
1. _____
2. _____
3. _____
4. _____
5. _____

Which of the two exercises was easier? I would imagine it was a whole lot easier to name the people who made you feel special than it was to remember the most powerful sermons that you've ever heard. Guess what? That's what the kids from your church will remember too! They won't remember the people in the congregation who had the most Bible knowledge, but they will remember the people who made them feel special and loved them.

Did you ever think what would happen if adults made the decision that every Sunday morning, they would do their best to make every student feel like they were the most important person in the world? Can you imagine what kind of impact it would make in the lives of our children if they knew that 20, 30 or even 50 adults really loved and cared about them? The result would be that those students would begin to see the church as the most loving place on earth.

Lead By Example

While making students feel loved and accepted is a really important part of making children matter at church, there are other steps that we can take to avoid favoritism and show students that they matter in our congregation. This next step involves the lead pastor.

The lead pastor will set the temperature for the importance of children in your church. That means if the congregation hears the pastor talking about how great children are, if they see him talking with students, listening to them, then most of the time they will follow his lead and the result will be that you will have a congregation that is full of children. However, if the lead pastor never talks about children or if he talks about students in negative ways, your church will reflect it.

I Couldn't Make This Up

About a year ago, my wife Vanessa and I went to support a new church plant on its opening day. We had been praying for this new congregation for over a year and couldn't wait to see how many people far from God were going to show up the first day. We drove to the church, parked the car, and walked inside the building with a few minutes to spare. After we sat down, we started talking to the people who were sitting beside us. We found out that they were also there as supporters for this new church plant.

As the service got started, the worship team sang three of four songs. There was a video and then they handed out visitor bags. Now this is where the story gets interesting. Inside the visitor bags was candy. Children love candy! So many of the kids in the worship center started to open the candy and eat it. Soon after they passed out the goodie bags, the pastor got up and started his message. About 20 minutes into his sermon, some of the children were still opening the candy wrappers and the pastor thought that the kids were making too much noise. So he stopped his message, looked at this little boy and screamed, "Stop making so much noise with that candy wrapper! Just open it up and put it in your mouth!" Then he said, "I can't stand kids. They drive me crazy. The only kids I like are my kids."

Vanessa and I looked at each other in total disbelief. I thought, "Did he seriously just say that? Did he just say that he didn't like children? Are you kidding me?"

The unfortunate part is that in many congregations, pastors view children the very same way. Now granted, most pastors would never verbally destroy a child in the middle of a sermon, but many kids grow up feeling very insecure around the pastors who lead the congregation.

That's why when I transitioned from student ministries to being a lead pastor, I made a very firm commitment. I promised myself that I would lead my congregation in such a way that I modeled true, Christ-like love for children. The reason I made that commitment was because I wanted the students at the churches I led to know how important they are to Jesus and to me. The only way they were going to see that was if we modeled it.

I have been a lead pastor for 8 years and have never waivered on that promise. I make sure that I talk to as many kids as I can on Sunday morning. I go on as many youth outings as possible. I write the kids from our church letters and send them in the mail. I text our junior high and high school students on a consistent basis to let them know I am praying for them.

The other thing that I do is no less than six times a year, I teach in our kindergarten to fifth program at Velocity. Their worship service takes place the same time as our adult service and six times every year, I teach the children in our church. The reason I do that is because if I am supposedly the best teacher/communicator at Velocity Church, then why wouldn't I give some of my time and talent to the people that Jesus said are the most important? Why would I only designate my teaching time for adults? Wouldn't that be a form of favoritism? After all, if Jesus, who was the best communicator of all time, gave some of His time to teach and love children, then why wouldn't I follow His example?

The truth is there are countless things that we as pastors can do to avoid favoritism and make children feel like the most important part of our congregation. We just need to start taking the steps necessary to make them feel like they are truly special and welcome.

CHAPTER 3

Actually, You Can Send A Boy To Do A Man's Job

If you've been around the church world for a while, you know that there are some stories that get told over and over again. They are the classics. I call them, "The Flannel Graph Heroes." They are parables about Biblical characters who did the most amazing things. They parted seas, built arks, interpreted dreams, saved nations, won beauty contests, and even saved entire races of people.

One of the most famous flannel graph heroes was a young man named David. Most people know him as King David. But before David became the king, he was nothing more than a shepherd boy. He spent his early years keeping watch over the flock. During that time, he developed a very useful skill that landed him a place in the palace as an adult. You see, when David was just a young boy, he became very handy with a slingshot. He must have stood in the fields for hours practicing over the years. He discovered which rocks fly the best. He figured out when to release the sling at just the right time in order to hit his target. Over time David became a very skilled marksman. As a matter of fact, Scripture tells us that he became so proficient that he was able to kill both lions and bears.

Interestingly enough, the skill that David learned as a child came in very handy when he was just a teenager. The Bible tells us that the Israelites were going into battle against the Philistines and the Hebrew people didn't think that they could win. Why? Because the Philistines had a warrior named Goliath. Goliath had been a warrior his entire life and this overgrown bully never lost a fight. Scripture tells us that every day this enormous slug would come out and challenge the armies of Israel to a fight by saying:

> ......"Why do you come out and line up for battle? Am I not a Philistine, and are you not the servants of Saul? Choose a man and have him come down to me. [9]If he is able to fight and kill me, we will become your subjects; but if I overcome him and kill him, you will become our subjects and serve us." [10]Then the Philistine said, "This day I defy the ranks of Israel! Give me a man and let us fight each other." [11]On hearing the Philistine's words,

Saul and all the Israelites were dismayed and terrified (I Samuel 17).

That was pretty strong talk. The Israelites must have thought that Goliath was big enough to back it up because not one man, IN THE ENTIRE NATION OF ISRAEL, was brave enough to face him. Every day he would stand in front of the Hebrew army doing his best to draw his line in the sand and pick a fight….and none of the Jewish men were willing to go toe-to-toe with him.

It just so happened that one afternoon David, this teenage shepherd boy, walked into the Valley of Elah. He showed up just about the time that Goliath walked out to spew his usual banter.

> David left his things with the keeper of supplies, ran to the battle lines and greeted his brothers. [23]As he was talking with them, Goliath, the Philistine champion from Gath, stepped out from his lines and shouted his usual defiance, and David heard it. [24]When the Israelites saw the man, they all ran from him in great fear.
>
> [32]David said to Saul, "Let no one lose heart on account of this Philistine; your servant will go and fight him" (I Samuel 17).

I would imagine that when this teenager popped off his comment, everyone must have shrugged it off. They must have thought, "Ha! Teenagers. They think they're so tough." Even Saul, the king himself, didn't think David stood a chance. That's why he said:

> [33]Saul replied, "You are not able to go out against this Philistine and fight him; you are only a boy, and he has been a fighting man from his youth" (I Samuel 17).

No one thought David had a chance to win, but David saw it differently. You see, David had a skill that Saul and his entire army didn't realize. David knew how to use a slingshot. He knew how to handle adversity. He'd done it since he was a child.

David walked over to the stream, chose five smooth stones and put them in the pouch of his shepherd's bag. Then he marched out to meet Goliath face-to-face. As he walked closer to the Philistine warrior, Goliath saw that he was only a boy and he began shouting obscenities at him.

David, like most teenagers, was really good at trash talking, so he fired back and told Goliath that not only was he going to kill him, he was going to cut off his head, and his posse was as good as dead. David ran toward the battle line twirling his sling and when he let go of the rock, it hit Goliath in the forehead and he fell to the ground.

Now I know what some of you are thinking. Some of you are thinking, "Okay, Scott. Thanks for the flannel graph story, but what's the point?"

The point is that young people can do far more than we think they can do. There wasn't a soldier in the entire army of Israel who thought David could have won that fight. Even the king doubted his ability, but this teenager shocked the crowd when he killed Goliath.

The Reality

The amazing part is that many people feel the very same way about kids today. Many churches never give young people an opportunity to do big things. Few churches would ever let young people lead worship. After all, they're just kids, right? We would never let them preach on Sunday morning. After all, they're just teenagers, what do they have to share? Many churches would never let young people take up the offering, pass out communion, serve on committees, write plays, create dances, or even be greeters at the front doors. Those spots are reserved for the truly gifted adults.

Or are they? Do we have an enormous amount of horsepower sitting in our pews week after week doing absolutely nothing? Are we keeping young people from developing their God-given potential because we think they are too young? That doesn't make sense to me.

I've seen teenagers memorize a 200-page script for a high school play. I know children who learn hours of music for a piano recital. I've witnessed students raise thousands of dollars, rent banquet halls, and put together an entire evening of fun and excitement for their homecoming and prom. Young athletes learn two or three different offenses and defenses for the sports they play. But for some reason, those same students are never asked to be an active part of the church until they reach a certain age.

What many pastors and churches don't realize is that there is a tremendous amount of talent and energy sitting in their building week in and week out. Young people can do far more than we could possibly imagine. One of my goals as a pastor is to challenge all of the students in our congregation to get involved in some area of service in the church. I don't care if they volunteer on the worship team, preaching team, greeting team, Kidz City team, or even the production team. I just want them to be involved in some type of ministry.

I would admit that with some of these students, I do have some ulterior motives. I don't want all of the best and brightest students to go into the marketplace to be millionaires. I want some of the best and brightest students in our congregation to go into some type of full-time ministry to impact the lives of other people. I want them to be missionaries to foreign countries. I want them to be lead pastors, youth ministers, worship leaders, and even church administrators. I want them to use their God-given gifts for the kingdom.

Boy Bands

Over the years, I have had the privilege of discipling some really great students and many of them ended up going into full time ministry. One of those overly talented students was a boy named Eric Hankins. I first met Eric when he was 12 years old. He was a short, pudgy kid who had a 1950's flat top and an addiction to boy band music. He loved singing the latest and greatest hits from the radio. I even have some rather embarrassing video to prove it.

When Eric was in 8th grade, I noticed he had some unique abilities. He was a natural born leader and he was a decent singer. So from the time he was in 8th grade I did everything I could do to show him that he could make a difference in the world. But I didn't just tell Eric that he could make a difference, I gave him the opportunity to make a difference.

When Eric was just a teenager, I started putting him in charge of all kinds of activities for our youth group. I had him make videos, lead small group sessions at camp, and even teach for me on occasion. Was he an outstanding communicator at first? Not really. But I would imagine that the first time David used his slingshot he wasn't a pro either. I would guess that if David had to fight Goliath after only a week or two of practice, that famous flannel graph story would have a different ending. I didn't care how good Eric was at the beginning. I believed that if he took the skills God gave him and if I gave him a chance to refine that talent, he could make a huge difference with his life.

After a few years of giving him opportunities in our youth group, I stepped it up a notch. Ten or fifteen times throughout the year, I would speak at different teen conferences or conventions. So whenever I would do an event for a teen conference, Eric would go with me. He didn't go as a spectator. I took him with me so he could deliver one of the messages. Weeks before I was scheduled to speak, I would tell him what my responsibilities for the convention were and I would say, "Okay Eric, in a few weeks we are going to a teen convention. I have four one-hour sessions to do that weekend and I want you to do one of them."

So when Eric was only 14 years old, he got the experience of speaking to thousands of other teenagers about different aspects of being a disciple of Jesus. He did a great job and it gave him an opportunity to start developing the gifts that God gave him. My thought was, "If he can start developing his skills when he is just 14, imagine how great he will be when he is 18."

I didn't allow Eric to just preach for me at conventions. He was also a decent singer, so I allowed him to lead worship at our church. We gathered about 4 or 5 teenagers who had some musical ability and I allowed them to lead worship (on main stage) at least 2 or 3 times a month. Were they outstanding? Not at first, but I was committed to allowing them to use their gifts regardless of their age. Over the course of several years, Eric developed into one of the best worship leaders I have ever seen. After he graduated from high school, he went on to Bible College to pursue a degree in Worship Ministry. Today he leads worship at a mega-church in Philadelphia.

The challenging part of allowing students to be so actively involved in the church, especially during the Sunday morning worship service, is that you will get push back from a lot of adults (and I know what I'm talking about). Every week, I had a steady stream of adults who blasted me with nasty emails. They called me on the phone every

Monday to complain. They would stop me after service to whine about "the noise that these kids were making with their drums and guitars." It was nothing less than brutal. To be honest, there were days when I dreaded answering the phone or even opening my emails.

Puff the Magic Dragon

Once I had a lady in her late 50's storm into my office one Monday morning. She was so mad I thought she was going to snort fire out of her nose. She looked like Puff the Magic Dragon. She walked through the threshold, slammed the door, and screamed, "Scott, you are ruining this church! You need to be teaching these kids how to serve us, not play music or be greeters on Sunday!"

I'm not one to yell or scream or throw things at people when I get angry. But this lady's comment revealed how she really felt about students and I got really upset. So I said (in the nicest tone I could muster), "Well, I actually disagree with that. I don't think that the church is a place for kids to serve you. I think this is a place where we as adults disciple students and allow them to develop the gifts that God has placed inside of their hearts."

She didn't like my response, and since she didn't get the answer she was looking for, she tried another method. She said, "You know Scott, I will make you a promise. If you do what I want, this church will never have money problems….and you won't either."

Remember when I said that I don't yell when I get angry? This was one of those times I did. I was so furious that I looked across my desk and said, "I think this church is going to have money problems for a long time because there is no way that I'm going to stop allowing our students to develop and grow here. Secondly if you think that your money is going to persuade me, you are out of your mind! So do me a favor and don't let the door hit you in the rear end on the way out!"

She didn't like that answer either. Two weeks later, she left the church. So did 30 other adults. They didn't get their way, so they took their ball and went home. Do you know what I did? I chalked it up as a blessed departure and allowed those students to keep developing their gifts. The part about those adults leaving that still bothers me is that they missed the opportunity to be a part of a church that allows young people to get involved and use their God-given abilities.

If you really want to make children matter in your congregation, then you must allow them to develop and use their natural abilities. If they have the ability to lead, let them lead. If they can sing, let them sing. If a teenager is amazing with sound and lights, let them use that God-given ability at church.

Watching students sit in a pew week after week does not facilitate any kind of development. All that does is teach them that it's okay to be a neutral bystander when it comes to serving. If you really want to impact the next generation of young people, and if your church truly wants to make children matter, then your congregation needs to equip them, train them, and allow them to be active players in the church.

CHAPTER 4

Put Your Money Where Your Mouth Is

Right after I graduated from Bible College, I took a youth ministry position at a church in lower Appalachia Kentucky. The church was located.... well....in the middle of nowhere. It was an hour and a half to the nearest major city. This town was so small that it had no stoplights and only one intersection. In fact, the only amenities that this town had were a small grocery store, a hardware store, a volunteer fire department, a ten-table diner, and a funeral home. That was it! There were no hotels, no fast food, they didn't even have a police department. If I remember correctly, I think the zip code was E I E I O.

Even though this was a really small town, I loved working at that church. I spent seven years working as the youth minister of that congregation and I enjoyed every minute of it. The people were wonderful and they treated me like family (even though I was a Yankee). Throughout my seven-year ministry with that church, I saw God do all kinds of amazing things. There were hundreds of children and teenagers who gave their life to Christ and got baptized. We saw that youth ministry grow from 2 kids to over 100, and that was in a town of 800 people!

As great as that experience was, there was one thing that always bothered me. What annoyed me was the amount of money the church allocated in the budget for the youth ministry. When I worked at this church, we averaged a little over 300 people a week at our Sunday morning worship service and 100 of those people were students. You would think that if almost one-third of a church consisted of young people the budget would reflect that. It didn't. Our budget for the entire youth program (K-12th grade) was less than $100 per week.

The sad part of that story is that it's not unusual. Most congregations do not designate huge portions of their budget for student ministries. According to one ECCU study, most churches only allocate 3% of their budget for children and youth programs.[1]

George Barna did a study that concluded that 41% of the people who attend an evangelical church on a normal weekend are under the age of 18. However, less than 15% of the average church's budget is dedicated to the needs of children's ministry.[2]

While many pastors and congregations say that student ministries are important, their budgets don't reflect it. Churches will spend big bucks on sound systems, lights, LCD projectors, glass bead screens, and the latest software for their worship services. But when it comes to budgeting for children's programming, kids often get the leftovers.

Window of Opportunity

Whenever I am asked about why budgeting is so important when it comes to student ministries, I often point people to the 4-14 Window. The 4-14 Window was a study done several years ago which revealed that in the United States, nearly 85 percent of people who make a decision for Christ do so between the ages of 4 and 14.[3] In other words, the majority of people who give their life to Christ do so between the ages of 4 and 14. If people do not accept Christ as their Savior before they reach their teenage years, the chance of them doing so literally falls off the charts.

The 4-14 Window isn't the only factor. A huge portion of the world's population (nearly 2 billion) is made up of individuals under the age of 18.[4] Now, let's put this into perspective. If the 4-14

Window is true, and if 2 billion people are under the age of 18, then why wouldn't we spend vast amounts of resources on the people who represent the biggest opportunity for evangelism? Why wouldn't we pour out our time, talent, and treasure into the group of people who would not only give us the best return on investment, but on the people that Jesus said are most important?

The Truth That's Never Been Told

One of the reasons that many churches don't invest in student ministries is because they don't see young people as a critical part of the church. They would never admit that, but it's true. Many church leaders and pastors view student programs as nothing more than a vehicle to attract adults to their Sunday morning service. I couldn't tell you the number of pastors that I've met over the years who have said, "If we want to attract families into our church, then we need to have stuff for their kids." Now what they were saying *sounds* spiritual. It sounds like they are saying that children matter. It even sounds like something a pastor, elder, or church leader should say.

But the reality of their message is this: "If we want to get a bunch of adults in here on Sunday morning to see our band and listen to the message, then we've got create something for kids. After all, the more adults we can lure to church through kids programs, the more adults we will have in our service. The more adults we have in our service, the better our numbers will look and the more money will come in during offering."

Sound absurd? Maybe. But it's closer to the truth than a lot of pastors would care to admit. To some church leaders, children are nothing more than a means to an end. But children are NOT leverage! They are people! Real people! They have thoughts and hopes and dreams and they want to know and understand the truth about God's love just like every adult does.

If we really want to be able to say that we are making children matter in our churches, then we need to put our money where our mouth is. If we say that children matter in our churches, then our budget needs to reflect it. One of the biggest ways we are going to make an impact on the young people in our churches and truly reach this generation for Christ is by investing Kingdom money into the lives of children.

Jesus put it like this, "Where your treasure is, there your heart will be also" (Matthew 6:21). What Jesus was saying is what you spend money on reflects what you truly value. If you value sports, then you will spend money on season tickets. If you love hunting, fishing, or scrapbooking, then your checkbook will reflect that. If a church would say that they truly love and value children, then it needs to be reflected in the budget. Churches that really want to make children matter will invest in it financially. They will spend Kingdom dollars on the people that Jesus said are the most important in the Kingdom.

That Doesn't Mean…

Investing financially in the lives of young people doesn't mean that we allocate a few more dollars for VBS or Goldfish® crackers. It doesn't mean that we throw a coat of paint on the walls of the youth room and think that we've really outdone ourselves.

Investing in the lives of children is a lifelong, day in and day out process that never stops. Investing in the lives of children means that we constantly recruit and train volunteers who are equipped to help children understand the truth about God's love. It means that we invest in our children and youth volunteers by sending them to training seminars and conventions. We spend money to train them in the most effective methods in reaching kids who are far from God.

It also means that the church pays the children and youth ministers well. I spent 14 years in student ministry and I could honestly say that most student ministers (children and youth) are the most overworked, underpaid, servants in the Kingdom. Many of them make such meager incomes that they can barely afford to put gas in their car. And the worst part is that some of those underpaid pastors have to pay money out of their own pocket for curriculum, events, camps and even basic supplies because they don't have enough money in their budget.

We Can't Afford It

When it comes to children and youth ministry budgets, I've heard a lot church leaders say, "We would like to budget more money for our student ministries, but we can't afford to do that right now. We'd like to, but we can't." When it comes to student ministries, you can't afford *not* to invest in them. Every year there are thousands of children and teenagers who could be reached with the message of Jesus if we would just allocate the necessary resources.

Back in 2009, when I was getting ready to start Velocity Church, I wanted to do things differently. I wanted to create a church that lost people would love to come to and I wanted to create a church where children truly mattered. I knew that the only way those two things were going to happen was if we planned for it, prayed for it, and if our budget reflected it. So when I was planning our budget, I allocated a huge portion of resources to those two things. Five years later, our church has grown significantly and we have helped hundreds of people get reconnected with God. But one of the things that I'm happiest about is that a little over one-third of our church is made up of children and teenagers.

When people ask me, "Scott, how do we know if we (as a church) are really making children matter?" I ask them two basic questions. The first question I ask is, "What is the total budget for your church?" The second question I ask is, "How much of that budget is designated for children and youth ministries?" The answer to those two questions will define how much you truly value children in your church. If you think it doesn't come down to money, you are wrong. Where your treasure goes, your heart follows. If you really value children in your church, then your budget will reflect it.

1. Schulz, T. (2013, August 6). The Shocking Truth of Church Budgets. Holysoup.com. Retrieved December 11, 2013, from
http://holysoup.com/2013/08/06/the-shocking-truth-of-church-budgets/

2. Barna, G. (2003) Transforming Children Into Spiritual Champions. Ventura, CA: Regal.

3. Kilbourn, P. (1996, June) Children in Crisis: A New Commitment. Lafayette Hill, PA: Marc.

4. Brewster, D. (2005, August). The "4/14 Window: Child Ministries and Mission Strategies. Compassion.com. Retrieved January 1, 2014, from
http://www.compassion.com/multimedia/The%204_14%20Window.pdf

CHAPTER 5

Home Sweet Home

One afternoon I was talking with a couple of high school sophomores in our church whose names are Kyle and Chuck. They told me that they always wanted to go to a rock concert, but they never had the opportunity to go. What they said didn't really surprise me. After all, there are a lot of young people who've never been to a concert before. We talked for several minutes and then I asked them what kind of music they listened to. I was desperately hoping that they weren't going to tell me that they liked some teenybopper group like One Direction or Back Street Boys.

To my surprise they said, "We like Metallica, AC/DC, Kiss, Ozzy Osborne, you know, bands like that."

"Do you like Motley Crue?" I asked.

"We love Motley Crue!" they responded enthusiastically.

I said, "Okay, I will take you to a Motley Crue concert the next time they come to Ohio."

Before I tell you the rest of this story, I have something I have to admit that I have never told anyone before. I'm not sure what you will think of me after I tell you, but here goes….I think Motley Crue is the best band ever. It's true. I have all their CD's. I've been to see them in concert over ten times. I listen to their music while I run, bike, ride in the car, and even when I mow the lawn. I've read all of their books including The Dirt, Tommy Land, The Heroin Diaries, and This Is Gonna Hurt (to be honest, I've read The Dirt three times).

A few months later, I found out that one of the stops on the Crue Fest Tour was going to be at Blossom Music Center, which is not too far from where we lived. I have a friend who is able to get really good seats for that venue, so I called him to ask if he could get me three tickets for the show. Unbelievably, he was able to get three front row seats to Crue Fest. I couldn't believe it.

I didn't tell Chuck or Kyle where we would be sitting, but I did tell them that I was able to get tickets for the show. On the night of the concert we drove to Blossom, parked the car, walked into the pavilion, and headed toward the front of the stadium. When we got to security, I handed Kyle and Chuck their tickets and they couldn't believe where our seats were located. They were completely ecstatic. We laughed, screamed, and cheered for over two hours that night. I don't know if I've ever been to a better performance.

Toward the end of the concert, Tommy Lee sat down at a grand piano and began to play the intro to one of my favorite Crue songs, *Home Sweet Home*. As we stood there singing along with the band, I looked over at these teenage guys and thought, "It's a shame that this song isn't true for them. Their homes are anything but sweet."

You see, Kyle's mom left when he was just a couple years old, so when he was just a little boy, he went to live with his dad. His dad was an alcoholic who got remarried to a cocaine-addicted stripper after he divorced his first wife. Kyle's stepmom wasn't just a coke addict who took her clothes off for a living, she was also one of the most mentally and physically abusive people I've ever known. She is so sadistic that when Kyle was five years old, she tried to cut his fingers off with a pair of scissors because he touched something that "belonged to her." Fearing for his wellbeing, Kyle's grandparents adopted him and he's lived with them since he was six years old.

Chuck didn't have it much better. He also lived with his grandparents because his dad left when he was four and his mom was sent to prison for embezzling hundreds of thousands of dollars and for forging checks. Needless to say, both of these teenagers had home lives that were anything but sweet.

That night, after I dropped them off, I was driving home and I realized something that I had never thought about before. As a matter of fact, I hadn't thought about it until the night of that concert. I realized that one of the most unusual things from all my years as a student pastor is that I never really worked with "church kids." The bulk of my students were what I call "city kids" and the vast majority of them did not have a home-sweet-home situation.

The students in my children and youth ministries were an eclectic group of raging hormones that often had no spiritual guidance at home. They had no filter and would often say things that would make me scratch my head and wonder, "Are they being serious?" Let me give you an example.

A few years ago, I was standing in the worship center after our Sunday morning service and one of the girls in our youth group walked up and told me that she needed to ask me a really important question. We walked to the side of the worship center and she asked, "Scott, is it wrong for me to make out with another girl just to turn my boyfriend on?" She wasn't trying to be offensive. She wasn't asking that for shock value. She really wanted to know.

You see, many of the kids that I have worked with over the years were never taught basic morality. They came from homes that had very few rules. The only rules that many of them had were: 1) don't get pregnant and 2) don't get caught. Their parents didn't play an active role in their discipleship or their spiritual wellbeing. The only role their parents did play was the few brief moments when they gave them really horrible advice.

Do My Drugs

Over the years, I've had at least 20 teenage guys who have told me something to the effect of, "Well, my parents told me that if I'm going to do drugs, then I should use their drugs because that way they will know where it came from and I will be safe." Whenever a teenager would tell me that I would think, "Yeah, that makes sense....because I'm sure that your dad's drug dealer is an upstanding citizen. I'm sure he pays taxes and has probably been nominated for a Nobel Peace Prize."

I can't even count the number of teenage girls who have told me that their mom put them on birth control because they want to "protect them." The problem was that, in reality, they weren't protecting them. What those parents were doing was giving their daughters a green light to share their body with any guy they dated. It's a common occurrence that happens far too often with teenage girls.

The sad part is that many people are completely oblivious to the situations that the children and teenagers in their church come from. They think that all the kids in their congregation come from good homes. They are tempted to believe that they have good parents, strong moral values, live in a decent house, in a nice neighborhood, and that they have plenty of food since both parents work a steady job. That's not true. Many of the young people in our churches come from some of the most broken and busted up situations that you could possibly imagine.

The Phone Call

One Tuesday morning, I was in my office working on my sermon when my cell phone rang. I picked it up and said, "Hello, this is Scott."

"Scott, this is Britney. I've got some really bad news. You need to go over to Amy's. Something happened. It's really bad this time."

As a pastor, you get phone calls all the time. Some of the calls are great. People are excited to tell me about answered prayer or that they are "expecting." But very few students ever called me to tell me how awesome they are doing. Most of them call when things aren't going well. Being in student ministry for over a decade, I got phone calls like that all the time. Calls about bad home situations, drugs, students being arrested, pregnancy, porn addictions, probation, etc.

That was the kind of call I got that Tuesday morning. The phone call from Britney didn't surprise me. She was really good friends with Amy - and Britney knew that Amy's home life was far from perfect.

Amy was a 7th grade girl whose dad bolted when she was a baby. Her mom had a steady stream of unhealthy relationships because she would meet a guy, fall in love, and within two weeks of dating they would move in together. As Amy was growing up, her mom had a revolving door of men who came in and out of their lives.

Amy lived with her mom, one of her mom's newest boyfriends, and several younger brothers and sisters. They weren't a well-to-do family. They lived in an apartment complex in an area that many people considered "the projects." They had very little money and food was a luxury.

Amy never led on that her home life was horrific. As the matter of fact if you met her, you would never know. Amy was a super cute, outgoing girl who had that rare magic of making people feel special just by being around her. She was invited to our church by one of her friends and Vanessa and I fell in love with her immediately. She was just one of those infectious people that everybody loved to be around.

That's why the phone call bothered me. I could tell by Britney's voice that this time something really was wrong. This wasn't just another fight between Amy's mom and her newest boyfriend. This wasn't another phone call to tell me that Amy hadn't eaten in a few days. Britney's tone sounded serious, almost frantic.

After I hung up the phone with Britney, I immediately left the office, got in my car, and drove over to her apartment. When I arrived, I got out of the car, walked up the steps to her apartment, and knocked on the door. I waited for several minutes, but no one answered. So I started driving around town looking for her, but Amy was nowhere to be found.

Several hours later, I finally tracked her down. As soon as she saw me, she put her head down and started to cry like she had done something wrong. I walked up to Amy, put my arm around her shoulder and asked, "What's going on?"

Amy was always honest with me. So she began to tell me what happened and it was a story that I wish I could forget. She told me that her mom left for work early that morning and she was alone in her apartment with her mom's new boyfriend and her little brothers and sisters. While Amy was getting ready for school, the boyfriend wandered into her room. He spent the next 30 minutes trying every persuasive tactic in his arsenal to convince Amy to have sex with him. She said, "Scott, there is no way in hell I would ever do that. So when I kept telling him no....he grabbed me and tried to force me on my bed."

Left with no other option, Amy did what she had to do. She hit him in the face and ran out of the house. Tears streamed down her face as she ran down the road. Amy walked into a convenient store and called Britney to tell her what happened and that's when I got the phone call.

I told Amy that she needed to call the police and tell them what happened. She did. Within minutes, two squad cars pulled in the apartment complex. They questioned Amy for over an hour about what happened. As I stood in the apartment listening to Amy answer questions that no 13-year-old girl should ever have to answer, my heart just broke.

Unfortunately, the story doesn't end there. What happened to Amy was enough to crush the spirit of any 7th grade girl, but what happened later that day was even worse. The police called Amy's mom at work and told her that she needed to come home. About 20 minutes later, Amy's mom pulled into the complex. She got out of her car, walked up the steps, opened the door, and exploded into a furious rage. She immediately started yelling at the police, "What are you doing here? Where are my kids? You need to get out of my house! I have rights you know!"

The police started to explain what happened and that's when all hell broke loose. You see, Amy wasn't the only one who went running out of the apartment that day. Her mom's new boyfriend also left. He packed up his stuff and ran out of the apartment. He didn't bother to find someone to watch the younger children. He just left them home alone….for five hours.

When Amy's mom found out that her boyfriend wasn't there, she blamed Amy for being the reason that he left. She also told Amy that she had to leave. She couldn't live there anymore. She would have to find a new place to stay or go to an orphanage. Needless to say, Amy was devastated. Being 13 years old and homeless is not the ideal situation. Fortunately Amy was taken in by some relatives, but her life was never the same.

You probably wouldn't be surprised if I told you that there were Amy's in every city, but there are also Amy's in every church in America. They are the children and teenagers who come to our churches from environments that most of us could never even imagine and do you know what they need? They need you! You can make a difference in their life!

Me? What Can I Do?

Most Christian people, especially in America, view helping young people in terms of giving money to a cause. They think that if they throw a few bucks to some kid-centered non-profit organization that they are really making a difference. In some cases, they might. After all, there are a ton of non-profits that need monetary resources to run programs and meet legitimate needs.

But what I've seen over the past 20 years is that way more students need someone to disciple them, than they need another program. Young people need an adult who is willing to invest some of their time to show them that they are loved, gifted, and that they truly matter. Why couldn't you "spiritually adopt" one of those kids? Why couldn't you find a young man in your congregation whose home life is horrible and go to some of his basketball games just to cheer him on? Why couldn't you spiritually adopt a little girl who doesn't have a dad and spend an hour with her every week? Why couldn't you support her by going to her elementary school band concerts and watch her play the flute? Why couldn't you be the one to invite them over for dinner, take them to a concert, show them how to change a flat tire, write a resume, or even the basics of finances?

The most common reason many Christians don't invest in the life of a child is because they say that they don't have the time. We have plenty of time for watching hours of television, surfing the web, posting meaningless banter on Facebook, and watching countless hours of video on YouTube. But when it comes to the broken children in our own church, in front of our own eyes, many people say that they just don't have the time.

The reality is, just like money, you will give your time to what you think is most important. If you think that Monday night football is important, then you will box out four hours every Monday in the fall to watch the game. If you think that reading a mindless novel is important, then you will notch out blocks of time to read. Whatever you think is most important is where you will spend your time. So the real question is - are the students whose home lives are all messed up worth some of your time? The answer should be yes.

Jesus Loves You

We have a woman in our church whose name is Debbie. She is a lady in her early 40's and she has a number of health problems. Some of her health problems are so severe that many days she can't even get out of bed, but Debbie is an unusual person. I don't mean that her personality is unusual. What I mean is that she is one of those rare individuals who sacrifices her time for hurting children.

When Debbie was just a teenager, her family fostered a boy named Ryan. Ryan spent considerable time at Debbie's house growing up and she treated him like a member of the family. They would play catch, watch TV, and spent a lot of time together. As Ryan became an adult, he got totally engrossed in the world of chemical addiction and got addicted to crack cocaine. When Ryan got older, he had two children with the woman he was dating. But even the love he has for his children couldn't break his addiction. These two infants live in a world that most of us could never understand.

That's where Debbie comes in. Every week, Debbie will drive several miles to pick up Ryan's two little children, and even though she isn't in good health, she brings these two kids to church every week. She told our small group, "I have to do this. This may be the only chance that these two children will ever have to learn about Jesus."

Debbie isn't just making an impact on these two children. She's making an impact on me. One Sunday, when I finished my message, I sat down in the front row and prepared to take communion. Debbie was sitting behind me with Ryan's two-year-old little boy on her lap. As she took communion I heard her whispering very quietly in his ear, "Jesus loves you. Jesus loves you." As I sat there listening to her encourage this little boy I thought, "Here I am *talking* about Jesus and there she sits *being* Jesus."

How amazing would it be for the students from broken homes to have someone like Debbie in their life? How great would it be for them to learn what it means to have a great marriage because they spent time with you and your spouse? How awesome would it be if these children learned to pray, understand Scripture, or even how to share their faith? All those things are possible if you would just give them some of your time.

The best place for the most broken young people in our society to go is to an environment that is filled with adults who love and cheer for them in spite of all their issues. The church should be that place. The church should be the kind of place where we welcome the wrecked and bless the broken. If we would just take the time to invest in the life of a child, then we could literally change the course of human history.

Shelly's Story

Shelly's home life was far from perfect. She was one of the countless girls in my youth group who was a victim of an absentee dad and her mom was a functioning addict. Since Shelly's home life was atrocious, she spent the majority of her middle school and high school days trying to find the love that she never got when she was a little girl. She wasn't bad, she was just broken.

Vanessa and I met Shelly when she was 15 years old under very unusual circumstances. Our church rented out a theater for a Christian-based movie and I challenged all the kids at our church to invite a friend to the film. Shelly was invited to the movie by one of the girls in my youth group whose name is Mandy. Mandy didn't know Shelly that well, but they had English class together, so Mandy just asked her to come. At the end of the film, one of the students in my youth group stood up and talked about how God can truly change your life. That night Shelly gave her life to Christ and was baptized.

Throughout the course of her high school days, Shelly spent a lot of time at our church. She was an active part of our youth group and all the adults just fell in love with her. Through the years, we got to know more about Shelly's home life and her story. As a result, several of the adults in the congregation decided to adopt Shelly spiritually. They would write her notes and send them in the mail. Others would invite her over to their house for dinner.

After Shelly graduated from high school, she decided to go to college to become a teacher. She worked two and sometimes three jobs to put herself through school because she didn't have any financial or emotional support from home. What she did have were the adults from our church who loved and cared about her.

Several times a month, Shelly's spiritual mentors would give her money to help offset some of her costs for college. Every time they would give Shelly money, she would have the most peculiar look on her face and would ask, "Why do you guys keep giving me money?" The answer was always the same. People would say, "We just want you to know how great we think you are and how much we believe in you."

One day I got a phone call from one of the men in our church and he said, "Scott, I want to buy Shelly a car. I saw her vehicle in the parking lot on Sunday and nobody should be driving a car like that. So I'm going to buy her a car and you are going to give it to her. I don't want you to tell her who it's from because I don't want her to know. Just give her the keys and tell her how much we love her."

A few weeks later, this man dropped off a car at my house. I called Shelly and told her that I needed to see her and it was important. When she got to my house, I handed her the keys to the car and told her that we wanted her to know how much we loved her. She cried….a lot. Shelly couldn't believe that anyone could love her that much.

Eventually Shelly graduated from college and got a job working with autistic children at a Christian school. I asked her recently, "Where do you think you would be today if it weren't for the people from that congregation who loved you?"

She said, "Before I came to church, I was so wrapped up in drugs, alcohol, and making the wrong decisions that I honestly believe that I would have hurt myself in such a way that I couldn't recover or that I would be dead. Just thinking about where I would have been makes me even more grateful for Mandy, the church, and all the people who showed me what unconditional love really is."

Stories like that are very possible in your church too. It's not a complicated process. All you have to do is find a young person whose life is completely broken and invest your love and some of your time…and trust me when I say that there are kids just like Kyle, Chuck, Amy and Shelly in your church too.

Section III: City

Would Anyone Notice?

There's a question that has been rolling around my mind for the past five years. It's a question that scares me to the core of my soul. As the matter of fact, if my suspicions are right, I think we're in big trouble.

"What's the question?" you wonder. Here it is: If someone picked up your church and moved it out of your city and placed it in another city – what would the city you left lose? Let me say that again. If someone picked up your church building and made all the people in your congregation leave the current city that you were in and move to another city – what would the city you left lose?

Would the city lose anything other than your Sunday School, worship service, and yearly VBS? Are the only things that the city would lose the religious services that you provide on a weekly basis? Could you simply move to another location with very few people even noticing that you had gone?

Or would the fabric of your city be completely torn because your church left? Would there be a huge loss in the amount of people who cut grass for the elderly? Would single moms who are struggling to make ends meet notice the difference? Would the school system go into a state of panic because all of their best volunteers who help children learn to read have gone? Would there be a frantic search for Little League coaches that truly love and nurture children through sports? Would the city feel the effects of your church leaving because there would be no one to visit the elderly, counsel the inmates, or to be a mentor to the most troubled teens?

My suspicion is that in most cases, the cities in which our churches reside would not lose very much. To be honest, I think that most cities would not lose one thing as the result of some churches leaving town. Do you want to know why? Because for some reason, most congregations don't think externally. They don't think about the hurting, the helpless, and the hungry. Most churches think internally. They think in terms of buildings, baptisms, and budgets.

Seldom have I been a part of an elders meeting where the needs of the city are addressed. We spend countless hours talking about carpet, paint, and resurfacing the parking lot, but rarely will we talk about the true needs of our city, let alone the children in our city.

When was the last leadership meeting that you took 20 minutes to discuss what's really going on in your city or school system? When was the last time the elders, deacons, or even pastors asked tough questions like, "What's the name of the most hurting family in our city and what can we do to help them?" Have we ever spared a few minutes in our spiritually illustrious meetings to talk about feeding the poor, clothing the naked, and being the true hands and feet of Jesus?

When was the last time the pastor got up front on Sunday morning and challenged the parishioners to volunteer in organizations like Boy/Girl Scouts, Little League, Big Brothers/Big Sisters, or spend some of their time at the elementary school making copies for stressed out teachers?

Could it be that we have become so internally focused that we have forgotten about the most hurting children in the very city in which we live? Have we created a horrific Christian subculture where our only conversation about truly hurting children is when we gossip about how bad they are during dinner? Have we become so focused on ourselves, our church, and our worship service, that if someone asked us, "What's the biggest need in the city?" We could not answer that question?

How can it be that there are so many people who say they follow Christ and yet our prisons are full, the hungry aren't fed, the poor are overlooked, and many children - in our own cities - feel like they have no hope? Have we become such consumers that the only thing we truly care about is going home after work and letting cable TV wash over our soul? Have we become people who are so engrained in our own selfish lives, that the most broken children in our city are nothing more than an afterthought? Could it be that our congregations consist of nothing more than consumers of religious goods? Has it become evident that we aren't making the strides we need to in order to truly impact the children in our cities for Jesus?

By the way, impacting the children in your city has very little to do with a hipster worship leader who wears skinny jeans. It has even less to do with rock star pastors who have the ability to wow and zow the crowd on Sunday morning. Impacting the city is far more than offering a few meager midweek programs that children can attend.

So let me ask you that same question again. What would the city lose if your church ceased to exist? Would the citizens of your city even notice? Would they even care?

If the answer to that question is painful, hang in there. There is hope. There is a remedy readily available to even the most off-course congregation. It's a remedy that Jesus modeled in the early part of his ministry. Look at what the Bible says in Mark 4:23.

> [23] Jesus went throughout Galilee, teaching in their synagogues, proclaiming the good news of the kingdom, and healing every disease and sickness among the people. [24] News about him spread all over Syria, and people brought to him all who were ill with various diseases, those suffering severe pain, the demon-possessed, those having seizures, and the paralyzed; and he healed them.

The Bible speaks of Jesus doing two very specific things. First, he preached the good news. Jesus took the time to teach people the truth about God's love. He knew that part of his responsibility was to communicate the message of God's love with power and clarity....but that's not all that Jesus did. He didn't just preach and teach. He didn't just offer the masses a time to come and learn about God's love. Jesus also met the needs of the most hurting people in every city that he went. He was actively involved in meeting the needs of hurting and broken people. Why should we (and our churches) be any different? Why shouldn't we be actively involved in meeting the needs of the most hurting in our city? Why shouldn't we focus on doing the things that Jesus did? If we are going to call ourselves "followers of Jesus" - then we need to do what Jesus did.

Throughout Section III, I am going to give you several practical ways that you can meet the needs of the most hurting children in your city. This isn't an exhaustive list of things you can do. These aren't the only ways to make an impact, but these methods will give you a starting line on how to make an impact on the children in your city.

CHAPTER 6

Now It's Personal

One of the most important things that I tell people who really want to make an impact on the children in their city is to start small. Don't quit your job and start a child-centered non-profit. Don't take out a second mortgage on your house and buy a building for after school programs. The easiest way to make a difference is by finding out what organizations are already doing great stuff for kids and simply volunteer. Somewhere in your city there is a government entity, scout troop, Little League, or some type of organization that is already making an impact on children. Most of them are in desperate need of volunteers. Start there.

You don't need 50, 100 or 200 people to go with you. Just find an organization in your city that fits your giftedness and ask to volunteer. The reason I bring up your giftedness is because if you aren't an athlete, don't volunteer to be a part of the wrestling program at the Boys and Girls Club. What will happen is that you will spend two or three weeks volunteering and you will hate it. Eventually you will quit and it will be another adult walking out of a child's life. I'm not saying that each time you volunteer it should be a lifelong commitment. What I am saying is that you can't make a big difference in the life of a child if you only volunteer three weeks and you dread being there.

Find an area that you are passionate about and simply ask to volunteer. If you love camping, volunteer for scouts. If you get excited about mentoring, then be a part of Big Brothers/Big Sisters. If you love to read, then volunteer a few hours a week at a local elementary school to help kids learn to read or recognize their sight words. If you are concerned about children's safety in their home, then volunteer to be trained as a guardian ad litem. (Keep in mind that the organization you choose may have a process you need to follow in order to get involved. Many organizations that work with students require their volunteers to fill out an application, get finger printed, and in some cases, may even require references before you can start serving.)

One of easiest ways to begin is by looking around your city or surfing the web to find a program that matches your passions and simply ask to volunteer. One of the things that I am very passionate about is sports. I love to run, bike, swim and I also enjoy playing volleyball. So when I moved to Cleveland, I found out that our local YMCA was looking for a volleyball coach to run a ten-week session that would teach kids the basics of volleyball. It was a no-brainer. I love volleyball and I love kids. It was a perfect match.

I spent ten weeks training 15 kids on the fundamentals of volleyball and we had a blast. I taught them how to pass, how to set, and how to hit the ball. I showed them how to run a basic 5-1 offense. It was nothing really advanced. I just taught the kids the fundamentals of the game and spent time encouraging them.

After every practice, I would have the children sit in a circle. We would talk about what they learned that night and if they had any questions. Most of the time, they never had any questions about volleyball. The questions they had were about me. They wanted to know about my life, my wife, my kids, and how I learned to play volleyball.

After I answered all their questions, I took a few minutes to learn more about them. I had a set of two different questions that I would ask them every week. Questions like, "What is your favorite movie and why? Who is your favorite music group or rapper? What is your favorite subject in school?" The reason I asked those questions is because I wanted them to know that I was interested in them as people more than I was interested in their skill on the court.

The last night of the session, I brought in pizza and drinks. We sat around a table and talked about what we learned over the past several weeks together. Toward the end of the evening, I went around the table and complimented each child and mentioned how proud I was of their achievements.

As we wrapped up our last night together, each one of those kids thanked me for being their coach. One little boy whose name is Devonte lingered around until most of the other children and parents had left. He walked up to me and asked, "Scott, you told me every week that you thought I was special. Do you really think that?"

I looked at this ten-year-old boy and said, "Special? I think you are the most special boy in the world. I think you run fast and jump high. I think you are so talented. As the matter of fact, I think you could be the President of the United States some day."

"Really?"

"Heck yeah! Not only that, I think you could be the smartest person in your whole school. You could be the best leader the world has ever known. I think you are one of the most gifted people I have ever met."

When I finished talking Devonte got a huge smile on his face and said, "Okay, I just wanted to make sure." With that, he bolted out of the doors of the gym and headed up the steps. A few minutes later, his mom walked into the gym as I was cleaning up and said, "Mr. Pugh, can I talk to you for a minute?"

"Sure."

"I want to thank you for what you said to Devonte. He has been having a really hard time in school since his father and I got divorced. I think he believes that it's his fault that his dad left. What you said to him tonight meant the world to him, and to me."

Making children matter in your city isn't rocket science. It just requires you to honestly care about kids that you don't know, to encourage them, and for you to be willing to give them some of your time. When you follow those three simple steps, the most amazing things can happen….it can even lead to children giving their life to Christ.

Easter Egg Hunt

Every year, our city does an Easter egg hunt for children at the community center. Each spring, David Thorne and I volunteer to paint the faces of all the kids who come to the event. I can't explain how hard it is to paint a child's face when they are totally zipped up on jellybeans and chocolate. They are so hopped up on sugar that they can barely sit still while I am painting their face – it's hilarious.

One year, David and I were partnered to paint faces with a middle school girl whose name was Amani. Amani was a young African-American girl who had a big personality and an even bigger laugh. She was an absolute joy to work with that day. We spent several hours painting faces together and I would ask Amani all kinds of questions about her school, her family, and even questions about what she enjoyed doing in her free time.

I didn't see Amani again for several weeks. As the matter of fact, I didn't see her again until April 4, 2009. The reason I remember the exact day that I saw her is because that was the opening day for Velocity Church. I was standing in the hallway of the school building that we use for our worship services, and about 15 minutes before our first service started, Amani walked in. I was really happy to see her. I walked over to where she was standing and talked with her for a few minutes. Amani told me that she wanted to come to our opening Sunday because she wanted to see what our church was like. What made her being there even more special was that she was so committed to coming that she actually paid her brother to drive her to our church.

Amani didn't just come to Velocity on our opening Sunday, she paid her brother to bring her every week. Eventually her brother, Mugisha, got tired of sitting in his car for an hour while Amani came to worship, so one Sunday he decided to join her. After about six months of attending Velocity on a consistent basis, Amani's parents started coming to our church. A few months later, she gave her life to Christ and was baptized.

Amani was a freshman in high school when she made the commitment to follow Jesus and our entire staff was devoted to helping her grow in her faith. During some of our conversations, she told us that she really liked to sing. I suggested that she try out for our Sunday morning worship team and she did. It turned out that Amani is an exceptional vocalist. So, when Amani was 15 years old, she started singing on our worship team.

Throughout the course of her time in high school, we did our best to disciple Amani. We took her to camps and special events. We challenged her to learn how to play the guitar and to develop her musical ability. Over the course of just a few years, Amani started leading worship at Velocity on Sunday morning and did an outstanding job. After Amani graduated from high school, she went on to Cincinnati Christian University to major in worship. Amani now interns at Velocity every summer and she is one of the most talented young people I have ever known.

The reason I tell you Amani's story is because when you make the decision to make children matter in your city by simply volunteering, you will meet young people just like Amani. You will get to see the kind of impact you are making in the lives of children and you will see it on a consistent basis….and in my opinion – there's nothing better than that.

CHAPTER 7

Partner With The City

In every town there are mayors, policemen, community directors, and other leaders who honestly love and care about the children in their city. Many of these city officials run programs and events for kids on a consistent basis. They don't run these programs for popularity points, re-election, or even political reasons. They do these things because they honestly care about children.

Let me be clear about something. Not every counsel member, mayor, or community director will be passionate about children. Many of them have other dreams and plans that they want to see fulfilled. That doesn't make them bad people; it just means that maybe they aren't wired that way.

One of the best ways for a church to meet the needs of the children in their city is by partnering with local leaders and government entities.

Partnership with the city may not come easy. You will have to do some research and talk to a lot of city and government officials to find out which politicians are truly passionate about children. That's what I had to do when I moved from Canal Fulton to Cleveland to start Velocity.

High Point

Back in 2002, I went to work at a great church in Clinton, Ohio called High Point Christian Church. I was hired as the youth minister overseeing student ministries from kindergarten to 12th grade. When Vanessa and I first started that ministry, the church consisted of about 150 people. The next six years were nothing short of amazing. God allowed us to catch lightning in a bottle and in just a few years we grew from 150 to a little over 400. We had a ridiculously large youth ministry. Our children stuff was off the charts and I was surrounded by elders who really wanted to see the church grow and flourish. Vanessa and I felt so blessed to be a part of such a great group of people.

But in April of 2007, my entire life got turned upside down. Over the course of a couple months, I got a series of phone calls asking if I would be interested in moving to Cleveland, Ohio to start a church.

To be honest, my first thought was, "Cleveland…seriously? Nobody wants to move to Cleveland, Ohio. The weather is horrible, and even though I love the Browns, they never win." I'm not saying my thoughts were spiritual, but they were my initial, off-the-cuff reaction.

I told the folks on the phone that I would pray about their request to plant a church in Cleveland (which I had no intention of doing) and would get back to them. Deep down, I knew the real reason that I was completely uninterested in their proposal. The truth was, I never wanted to start a church. That was never one of my goals in life. As a matter of fact, starting a church was probably the furthest thing from my mind. I was already working at one of the best churches ever and we had so many great things happening that I had never even considered leaving. Besides not wanting to leave our congregation, I didn't know anything about starting a church. I knew more about off-track betting in Yemen than I did about church planting.

Despite my initial feelings, and through a series of events that you would never believe, Vanessa and I began to feel like God was telling us to move to Cleveland to start a new church. I really struggled with those thoughts because I couldn't understand why God would want us to go. We had no reason to leave our church or the people we loved just to move to Cleveland and start a church.

Over the next few months, I set out to prove that what I was hearing and feeling was incorrect, and that none of this could be from the Holy Spirit. Basically, I was determined to prove that God was wrong. Once I did that to my satisfaction, I could stop worrying about it and get back to doing what I wanted to do – pastoring the church I loved.

So, every week I would get in my car on my day off and drive from Canal Fulton to Cleveland. I wasn't driving to Cleveland once a week to go sight seeing. I was driving there to find out what was really going on in the city. During my visits I would meet with every mayor, police chief, city official, and any other leader who would give me the time of day. I would sit down with them and I would ask them this question, "What's the biggest need in this part of Cleveland?"

The answers varied from, "We are really committed to stamping out Styrofoam" or "We want to green the waterfront." After every meeting, I would drive home knowing more than ever that God wasn't calling me to Cleveland. There was no way I was going to spend my life stamping out Styrofoam or greening the waterfront. I'm not saying those things aren't important, but I'm not wired that way.

In early January 2008, I called the office of South Euclid Mayor Georgine Welo and I asked her administrative assistant to set up a time for me to meet with her. Two weeks later, I walked into her office and met Georgine for the first time. For over an hour, she talked with me about the city of South Euclid and she was more than kind. During the course of our conversation, she gave me some background information and asked if there was anything she could do for me.

I said, "Yes, actually I have a question for you. What's the biggest need in this city?"

When I asked that question, the floodgates of her heart came pouring out. Georgine has this huge vision for South Euclid and she started talking about caring for the poor, hurting families, and for children. Then she said, "Scott, if you are going to come to Cleveland to start a church, then come to South Euclid and do something to help our children."

When she said those words to me, I was completely astonished. We talked for a few more minutes and then I left her office. As I walked towards my car, I couldn't stop my mind from racing. "Why would she say that? Why would she bring up children to me? Of all the things that she could have talked about why did she talk about kids?"

As I was driving home that day, I knew without a shadow of doubt that I was moving to Cleveland to plant a church and I was going for two reasons. First, I was going to start a church that would help people understand the truth about God's love. The second reason was to start a church that made the children of the city matter. Georgine's words were exactly what I needed to hear. As it turned out, God wasn't wrong. In fact, He had never been more right.

Playground of Possibilities

Six months later, Vanessa and I left High Point and moved to Cleveland. I asked Georgine for places that I could personally start serving and meeting the needs of the children in the city. In typical Georgine-fashion (because she always has big stuff going on) she said, "In a few months, we are going to build a new playground at Bexley Park for the kids in South Euclid. We are calling it the Playground of Possibilities. We want to build this playground in one week, but it's going to take 2000 man hours and about 1000 volunteers to make this happen. I would love if you would be a part of this."

After she told me her vision for this new playground, I couldn't get on the phone fast enough to track down as many volunteers as I could. Why wouldn't I? Who gets the chance to be part of building an entire playground for children? How many times have you been offered an opportunity to be a part of creating a place where hundreds of children will laugh, play games, and spend time with their family? This was truly a once-in-a-lifetime opportunity and I wasn't going to miss out on it.

David Thorne and I spent several weeks calling all of the churches that we knew. We asked the lead pastors if they would send as many people as they could to South Euclid to help with the playground build. Every one of those churches agreed to send people to help with the project. By the end of two months, we were able to recruit over 80 volunteers who served a little over 700 hours for the project. As the matter of fact, some of the volunteers from Northwest Avenue Church gave up an entire week of vacation just to serve. It was one of the best kid-centered events that I have ever gotten to be a part of and I loved every minute of it. The great part is that I didn't have to come up with the idea. We didn't have to lead it, organize it, or administrate it. All we had to do as a church was partner with what was already happening.

I would guarantee that there are events just like that in your town. It may not be a playground build, but there is likely a plethora of events that your church could help with by partnering with the city. It could be as simple as helping the city organize the Memorial Day Parade, chaperoning events, or just sending volunteers to help meet a need.

Offer Community Service

Another way to partner with the city is by offering community service to troubled teens. Any student who breaks the law is usually given some type of community service by the judge or magistrate. The young people have to do their community service hours somewhere, so why not partner with the police department and clerk of courts to have them do their hours at your church?

The way our community service program came about is really interesting. After I had lived in Cleveland for a couple years, I became good friends with the chief of police whose name is Kevin Neidert. Kevin is one of the best people I have ever met. He's been in law enforcement for over 20 years and he has the best stories that I have ever heard (seriously - his stories are both crazy and hilarious). We became running partners a few years ago and trained for a couple half marathons together.

One day Kevin called me and asked if our church would be interested in offering community service hours for students who have gotten in trouble with the law. He explained that the way the program would work is any teenager who has service hours to complete would be required to come to our church office and work their court-ordered hours with us. I thought about his request for about six seconds and agreed.

Who wouldn't? Who wouldn't love having 60-100 extra hours of manpower each month? That's like having a free part time employee! Who wouldn't love getting to meet and develop relationships with the most troubled teens in their city? It's a no-brainer!

For the past few years, we have had students come to our office to help us put together events, do set up, help with city-wide events, run games, and even edit video. We have been able to develop some really good relationships with some of the students. As a matter of fact, we became such good friends with some of these students that (with permission from their parents) we even take them with us to meetings and church planting events like Kingdom Synergy Partnerships. It's a win-win situation.

Wait A Minute

Before we go on, I want to say something to those of you who are thinking, "Wait a minute. Are you telling me that you allow criminals and law breakers in your church?" Yep, we sure do. We also allow tax collectors and sinners. As a matter of fact, we welcome prostitutes, drug addicts and basically the most lost people on the planet, and the crazy part is we actually care about them.

If that's a problem for you, I would challenge you to take some time and rethink why your church exists. I would imagine that your church began on the premise of the Great Commission. You know, to seek and save the lost, to baptize the broken. That's why your church exists, right?

If reaching truly lost people isn't the reason your church exists, then I would encourage you to re-read the Scriptures. Jesus didn't spend time with religious people. He spent time with lost people and those are the people who should feel the most love and acceptance from us.

"What's Easter?"

Last year, a 16-year-old boy in our town got caught with a backpack full of pistols and a bag of cocaine. He was charged with possession of a controlled substance and an illegal weapons violation. He was sentenced to a short stint in a youth correctional facility. When he got out, he had to pay restitution and had to complete 120 hours of community service at Velocity.

Well, one afternoon he was at our office collating some handouts for our Easter service. He worked for about an hour and then he asked, "What's Easter?"

David answered, "What do you mean?"

"Easter. What is Easter?"

"Hasn't anyone ever told you what Easter is about?"

"No."

David got up from his desk, sat down beside this student, and for the next thirty minutes, he explained what Easter is all about. He told this young man about God's love, the problem of sin and how God loved the world so much that he sent his son Jesus to die on the cross so that we could be forgiven from our sins. When David finished talking, this teenager couldn't believe what he'd heard. He looked at Dave and said, "Man, that's like….the best news ever. Can I tell my mom about this?"

David responded, "Absolutely! If you want me to, I will come to your house and explain it to your mom with you."

Life-changing conversations like this happen every so often at Velocity and do you know why? Because even though a student may have a criminal record, they still matter to us. Could there be a better place for a young person to do community service than at a church? Is there a better environment for them to feel accepted, encouraged and challenged? I don't think so.

It's Possible

I've met a lot of believers (especially church leaders) who think that it's literally impossible to partner with the city. That's just not true. It is possible for you (individually) and your church (holistically) to partner with local city and government programs to make an impact on children. Start small. Be faithful with little opportunities and bigger opportunities will eventually come your way.

If a city leader tells you "no" - don't give up because you think it's just too hard. I've been told "no" a thousand times. There is a person of peace in your city who is passionate about children. Partner with him or her and doors will open with opportunities to meet more broken people than you ever dreamed possible.

CHAPTER 8

Throw A Party

I don't know anyone who doesn't love a good party. I'm not talking about the kind of party where you wake up in somebody's closet wearing nothing but one blue sock and Elton John sunglasses. (Yeah, I went to college too.) Most people just really enjoy getting together with friends and family to celebrate life, athletic events, birthdays, weddings, anniversaries, and babies being born.

One of the easiest things that a church can do to make an impact on the children of their city is to throw a party. I'm not talking about a little get together with cake and ice cream. I'm talking about inviting every child in your city to an all-out, no-holds-barred celebration that is filled with fun and excitement.

When we first started Velocity, I wanted to be the church that every person in the entire city of

Cleveland would look at and think, "They really love and value children." So what did we do? We threw parties for kids. Ten times a year, we commemorate the children in our city by creating these outrageous events that celebrate children. We don't put these events on for PR. We don't do them for mass marketing. We do them to let children know how great we think they are and how much they matter to us.

Kidz Spring Spectacular

One of the child-centered celebrations that we do every year is called the Kidz Spring Spectacular. We throw this party the first Saturday of spring break every year. One of the reasons that we do this event is because I know that the majority of children on Cleveland's east side aren't going anywhere warm for Spring Break. As the matter of fact, because of the weather in Cleveland, many of them aren't even going outside unless they are sled riding.

The other reason that we do Kidz Spring Spectacular is because a lot of the children who live in our city would never have the financial means to go to Disney World or some fancy theme park. So we host this program to try and bring some of the "Magic of Disney" to them.

The way the event works is that we rent our local high school gym for the entire day. We bring in inflatable slides, bounce houses, mazes, obstacle courses, etc. We also bring in every cartoon character that we can think of such as Sponge Bob Square Pants, Dora the Explorer, Mickey, Elmo, Cookie Monster, Cinderella, Sleeping Beauty, Batman, Captain Jack Sparrow - even Darth Vader makes an appearance.

In the gym, we offer over 20 games like ring toss, ball bounce, Wheel of Fortune, and bean bag throw. No matter if the child wins or loses the game, they still win. Every child gets a piece of candy at every game they play. There is also free food, face paint, as well as balloon artists. The best part of all is that the entire event is free for every child in the city. Every year, we have thousands of people who come to this event to spend time with their children and just have fun.

Partner With the Pros

The Kidz Spring Spectacular is just one of the events that we do for children. We also host different sport camps. If your town is anything like ours, sports are huge. Since we live in a sports-saturated culture, one of the ways that we wanted to make children matter in our city was to create free sport camps for kids. Every summer, we partner with a professional athlete or a professional sport team to run free camps for the kids in our city.

Why would a church do that? There are two reasons. The first reason is that taking care of your body is scriptural (Ephesians 5:29). As a matter of fact, Paul even says that physical training has value (I Timothy 4:8). So why not give kids an opportunity to learn about how to be active and take care of their body?

The second reason we offer these sport camps is because many of the children in our city could never afford to pay $300 (or more) to attend some type of athletic camp. So our thought was, "If children really matter and we think that taking care of your body is important, then why not host sport camps for free?"

Rock Hill

One of our most successful sports camps is our football camp, and here's how it got started. I got a phone call from a guy named Brian Jones who lives in Rock Hill, South Carolina. He called me and asked if I was interested in doing a free football camp for kids in Cleveland. He also told me that NFL tight end Ben Watson would be the one running the camp and all I had to do was get the children to the camp and he would do everything else.

If you think like I do, there are some offers that seem too good to be true. This was one of those offers. So I said, "Are you telling me that Ben Watson, a professional football player, wants to come to the east side of Cleveland and run a football camp for kids, and not only that, he's going to do it for free?"

"That's right," he said.

"So what's the catch?"

"There is no catch," Brian replied. "All you have to do is get enough kids to have a camp."

I heard what Brian was saying, but his proposal still seemed way too good to be true. After all, how often does something like this happen? I was more than suspicious, but I allowed the conversation to go on for several minutes. Then I asked Brian, "How did you get my name?"

He said, "I know a youth pastor in North Canton whose name is John Moores. I called him to see if he knew anybody in Cleveland who was doing great stuff for kids and your name came up. So I wrote down your number and gave you a call."

"And you've done these types of camps before?"

Brian said, "Yeah, Ben runs a football camp for the kids here in Rock Hill every year. He was just traded to the Browns and we thought that we could run a camp in Cleveland if we could get enough kids."

After forty minutes of conversation, I agreed to move forward with the idea. Still, I was a little nervous. I've heard of pro players who "sponsor" camps for kids and the only thing they do is show up on the last day of camp for 30 minutes to sign autographs. My other area of anxiety was that I had no idea who Ben Watson was, since I don't watch a lot of football.

After a little research, I found out that Ben Watson wasn't just a professional football player, he was a two-time Super Champion. Ben won two Super Bowls with the Patriots and then he was traded to the Browns. He wasn't just a pro athlete. He was one of the best football players in the world.

First Impression

Several weeks later, I met Ben Watson for the first time. We got together with Brian to work out the details for the camp, and I have to admit, I was impressed right away. It wasn't his football knowledge that made an impact on me, it was his character. Ben is the nicest person you'd ever want to meet. He didn't act like a superstar. He was just a guy who happened to play football for a living. As a matter of fact, I was surprised when he talked more about his own family, than he did about football.

During our lunch, Ben and Brian talked about how the camp would run, the kind of activities that would take place, and what they needed me to do. It took about seven months of planning to make the first football camp happen. I had to get fields reserved for the players, liability waivers, emergency medical forms, water stations, pre-registration, etc.

When the first day of the camp finally arrived, we had so many children show up that we stopped taking registrations. We had a limit of 200 kids from 2-6 grade and we hit that limit in about 20 minutes. Young people from all over Cleveland's east side raced to be a part of the Ben Watson Skills Camp.

While the attendance was great, the best part of the camp for me was watching Ben around the kids. Ben didn't show up on the last day for 30 minutes to sign autographs. He spent 3 hours a day for 5 days with the children and they were more than enamored. These kids were shocked that this Super Bowl-winning, professional athlete would run around the field chasing them, throwing passes, giving high-fives, and cheering them on.

Every day, Ben would teach the kids about the basics of football, but he also told them about God's love. On the last day of camp, Ben brought all the kids, coaches, parents, grandparents, and even the TV crew together, and for 20 minutes, he shared how God had changed his life. During his talk, he challenged the players and their parents to be more, do more, and believe more than they ever had. It was nothing less than sensational.

Before we go on, I need to tell you something that you will not believe. I have the ability to read minds. Not really….but I do know what some of you are thinking. Some of you are thinking, "If I had someone like Ben Watson call me on the phone, then I would run a free football camp for kids too. But I don't know a pro football player, so we can't do that."

Before you get angry with me, can I ask you something? Have you ever called a pro or college team and asked them to partner with you? Have you called the local high school coach on the phone and asked him to help you organize an event like this for kids? The reason I ask those questions is because there are probably former high school, college and maybe even pro athletes who live in your city that would be more than happy to volunteer.

Wesley Fluellen

About two years ago, I met a guy named Wesley Fluellen at church and I spent several minutes talking with him. A week or so later, I called him and asked him if he wanted to get lunch. He agreed, so we met downtown at a little café. During our meal, I asked Wesley to tell me about his background.

He told me that he grew up homeless (yes, homeless) in Cleveland. As a child, Wesley lived in an abandoned house and he would eat anything he could find. Eventually he became a ward of the state and was put in the custody of Children and Family Services where he experienced an enormous amount of emotional, mental, and physical abuse.

He started playing basketball when he was 13 years old. Wesley was a naturally gifted athlete, so when he started playing basketball it was second nature to him. He developed into an exceptional high school basketball player and was offered a full scholarship to Robert Morris University. Wesley was a four-year starter at Robert Morris. After he graduated college, he went on to play professional basketball overseas. Then in 2004-2005, he played for the Orlando Magic.

I knew when I met Wesley for the first time that he was a tall guy, but I had no idea that I was sitting at lunch with a former professional basketball player. Over the next several months, Wesley and I got to know each other and we developed a really good friendship.

As summer approached, I asked Wesley if he would be willing to run a free basketball camp for the kids in our city during the summer. Wesley was thrilled to be a part of a camp like ours. From his experience of growing up homeless, he understood how difficult, if not impossible, it is for many children to attend a camp that costs money.

The other great part about partnering with Wesley was that, when it comes to basketball in Cleveland, he knows everyone and everything. During the camp, he brought in college coaches, former college players, and even other professional players. All we had to do was handle the logistics. Wesley was awesome around the kids, probably because he's a big kid himself. He would laugh with them, talk with them, and he taught them the fundamentals of the game.

Somewhere in your city there is an athlete just like Wesley who would be more than happy to partner with your church to run a free sports camp for kids. The best place to start looking is in your own congregation. I would imagine that someone in your church has some high school or college sports experience. Start there. Ask if anyone knows a college or pro player. Call local colleges and ask them if they would be willing to come and do a two or three day camp for you. Making an impact on the children in your city through sports is very possible, but you have to be intentional to make it happen.

Generosity Feeds

Another type of party that a church can throw is a Generosity Feeds event. One of the biggest needs, in most U.S. cities, is many children don't eat on a consistent basis. My friend, Ron Klabunde, learned this lesson after he moved to the wealthiest county in America to plant a church. Ron discovered that even though he lived in the richest county in America, over 11,500 local children struggled with hunger.

When Ron learned how many young people in his city struggled with hunger, he knew he had to do something about it. Several months later he started a non-profit called Generosity Feeds. Generosity Feeds brings together people of all ages, as well as city and local organizations, to pack and provide food for hungry children.

Generosity Feeds now works with 1,200 families (approximately 3,600 children, parents, grandparents, and young adults) to help change the lives of children across Northern Virginia. Generosity Feeds also does events for different congregations across the country that want to eliminate child hunger in their city. (For more information about how to host a Generosity Feeds event go to: generosityfeeds.org.)

Social Issues

Sports and parties aren't the only things that a church can do to make children matter in their city. You can also get involved in many social issues that children deal with on a daily basis. One of the things that really bother me about schools (both public and private) is the number of kids who are victims of bullying. I don't think that any child should be afraid to go to school. I don't care how a student looks, dresses, what neighborhood they are from, or even the color of their skin, no child should be afraid to go to school. When a child goes to school in fear, their ability to engage in the learning process diminishes radically.

Since I am very passionate about this subject, I contacted our local middle school and asked them if we could partner with them to educate both students and parents on the dangers of social media, bullying, and sexting. The school agreed to meet with me to see what I had in mind. We met several days later and I laid out my plan.

I said, "We can start off the event by cooking dinner for every family in the entire school. We will have rigatoni, beans, bread, drinks, and a desert. Parents who have younger children won't have to worrying about childcare because we will provide childcare for every child from birth to 8th grade. We will make sure that every volunteer from Velocity is fingerprinted, background checked, and we will give you copies of all the results.

After dinner, we will bring in a professional stunt bike team who gives an outstanding message on bullying. When the presentation is over, we will have all of the students participate in different activities around the school that inform them of the harmful effects bullying has on the lives of others. We will also instruct them on using their cell phones wisely when it comes to what they text."

I went on to say, "While the students are involved in their activities, we will do something different for the parents. I have already contacted the Cuyahoga County Prosecutors office and they have agreed to send two of their prosecuting attorneys and one online investigator to teach parents how to keep their children safe online.

They also teach parents the best way to monitor their child's online and cell phone activities."

The school loved the idea, so we got to work and planned the event out in a lot of detail. We had a ton of Velocity volunteers who took off work, sacrificed their time, and did their best to run events and challenge students. We have done this program for three years, and while the program varies from year to year, the results are the same. Children and parents are impacted.

Why would a church do this? At Velocity, we believe that Jesus' words were true when he said that we should do to others what you would have them do to you (Matthew 7:12). So why wouldn't we care about bullying? I want kids to treat each other the way that they want to be treated. I believe that the Apostle Paul was right when he said our bodies aren't meant for sexual impurity (I Corinthians 6:13), so why wouldn't we take the time to educate Junior High students about the dangers of sexting?

Separation of Church and State

When I tell people how much our church works with our school system and local government, they often ask me, "How can a church work with the public school system? How can you partner with the city? What about Separation of Church and State?"

My answer is, "What about it?" We aren't there to deliver a sermon or convert everyone to Christianity. We are there to serve and make a difference in the lives of children. I don't have to preach a sermon, carry a Bible, or hand out salvation tracks in order to make an impact. After all, one of my (and your) responsibilities as a follower of Jesus is to make a difference in the lives of others, and that goes way beyond what happens on Sunday morning.

For far too long the church has relegated itself to only being a distributor of religious goods. They try to make their "big" impact one hour every Sunday morning. I'm not saying that worship and preaching aren't vitally important – they are – but that's not all the church can do. We can do more than sermon series, VBS, potluck dinners, and an occasional church picnic. The church has the ability to bring joy to a child's life by throwing parties like Kidz Spring Spectactular, Pictures with Santa, Drive-In Movie Nights, or other fun events and activities. The church has the power to help a child understand the value of being physically fit, treating others with compassion, and even keeping yourself safe online.

Why in the world would a church do all that for the children in their city? Why would we throw parties, plan sport camps, and host educational opportunities for children and parents? The answer is really simple – it's because children matter. What better way for a church to celebrate children than for us to throw parties, offer programs, and events for children and their parents. These types of events provide parents an opportunity to be more involved in the lives of their children, and all we had to do was create the environment for that to happen.

The Reaction

The hilarious part about throwing a party or hosting a sport camp is the reaction we get from parents. We have so many adults who are completely taken back by the amount of work that goes into these events and are astounded that they are free. Over the past few years, we have had at least 100 adults approach us during our events and ask, "Why do you do this? We see Velocity creating all kinds of great stuff for kids. Why does your church do stuff like this?"

Whenever a parent asks me that question, I always give them the same answer. I say, "Because I really believe that children are the most important people in the world, and if your kids had fun and learned something valuable, then I would consider this event a huge success."

If you could see the look of astonishment in parents' eyes when I say that, you would burst out laughing. They just can't believe that anyone, especially a church, would do something like this for kids, with nothing expected in return.

Recently I had a single mom walk up to me after our free Pictures with Santa event and she said, "Scott, I have come to every one of your events for the past four years. I'm a single mom and I work two and sometimes three jobs just to make ends meet. We never have money to go on vacation or even go to the movies, so we plan our fun events as a family around the events that Velocity does for the city. I could never say thanks enough for all that your church does."

The truth is I don't want Velocity to be known as the church that just has a ton of people who come to our Sunday morning service. I want to be known as a church that does great stuff on Sunday and who does great stuff for their city. Your church can do the very same thing. You can have an awesome worship service and make a difference at the same time. It takes time and a lot of hard work, but you can make it happen.

What I Wasn't Going To Tell You

The information that you are about to read wasn't in the first draft of this book, simply because I wasn't going to tell you. However, after my wife Vanessa read the initial manuscript she said, "Scott, you need to tell them the rest of the story."

The reason I wasn't going to share this material is because I didn't want to come off like some kind of know-it-all – because I don't know it all. I didn't want to appear like I was bragging because I'm not. The only thing I can tell you is that the better we have remembered to serve the children in our city, the bigger our blessings have been. So with that in mind, let me tell you the rest of the story.

Velocity Church has been unbelievably blessed over the past five years. Our school system partners with us in ways that I could have never imagined. Every year, we are invited to take groups of students on field trips and plan special events for the entire district. Our school system has been so gracious that they have even allowed our church to use school buildings and host events for free because they love what we do for children.

The city has been just as wonderful. We partner with the city in every event and activity that they do. They allow us to use rooms, buildings, parks, and they advertise our events on the city website and at city hall. There are city officials and directors who have become very close friends and we could not be more thankful for their partnership.

One of the most amazing things that has taken place over the past five years happened about three months ago. I was sitting in our office working on my computer when the phone rang. The man on the other end of the line said, "Scott, this is Tim Snyder and I am the campus pastor for a Division II college here in Cleveland. We are a Catholic college, but over half of the students on our campus are not Catholic or believers in any way. We want to start a worship service on campus for those students and I was wondering if Velocity would do it."

Needless to say I was in shock. How in the world does a church get an opportunity like that? After several minutes of conversation, I asked Tim how he got my name. He said, "There is a lady who works in the President's office who gave me your name. She told me that if we were going to do something to reach college students with the love of Jesus, then I needed to call Velocity because they do great stuff for the kids in our city."

The next week, Tim and I met to discuss the details of what he was looking to do. During our conversation I asked him, "Tim, what do you want to see happen at this university?"

He said, "I want every student at this college to understand who Jesus is and how to follow him."

That was all I needed to hear. Several weeks later we started a non-denominational worship service on that college campus and God has blessed it in crazy ways. We have had such success that the administrators can't understand why so many students are coming to that service. In fact, they are so shocked that they are featuring an article about Velocity in their school newspaper.

I tell you that story for one simple reason. The better we have remembered to serve the children in our city, the bigger our blessings have been. There is no way that I would have ever dreamed we would be so blessed as a congregation. The reason that I think that God is blessing us is because we are doing our best to make the children in our city matter….and there's no reason you can't do the very same thing. Yes, it's going to take time. Yes, it's going to take a lot of hard work – but the very same God who has poured out His blessing on us for making children matter could do the very same thing in your congregation.

Section IV: World

All The Children of the World

Jesus loves the little children,
All the children of the world.
Red and yellow, black and white,
They are precious in His sight,
Jesus loves the little children of the world. [1]

If you grew up in the church you might be familiar with that song. The lyrics were written by a preacher in Chicago whose name was Clare Herbert Woolston. He wrote that song because he wanted the kids in his church to know how much Jesus loved children. The words of that song couldn't be more accurate. Jesus really does love all the children of the world.

That's what we are going to discuss in this final section. The last chapter of this book is going to show you the easiest way to make children matter around the world. Before we get started, can I ask you for a favor? Since we've been together for several chapters, I would like to make a request: Please read the final chapter of this book.

The reason I'm asking this from you is that when I bring up the subject of making children matter in other parts of the world, some of you may be tempted to stop reading. You may be enticed to close the book, put it on the shelf and never pick it up again. Let me tell you why.

Almost any parent understands the importance of making children matter in their home. Most followers of Jesus would agree that there is a Scriptural precedence to make children matter in their church. You may have even thought of some ways you could make children matter in your city.

However, when it comes to children in other parts of the world, many people don't see the urgency to make them matter. We view those children differently. Many people see them as the kids who live in countries that we can't pronounce. They are nothing more than the poor unfortunate souls who were born on the wrong side of the hemisphere....but they are still children who matter, right? They are still the little people that Jesus loves and died for on the cross.

In this final chapter, you will learn the reality of what many young people are facing all over the world. There are millions of children across our planet who live in situations that none of us could ever imagine, and they need a hero. In this last chapter, you will learn how you can be that hero. So do me a favor and keep reading.

1. Christiansen, R. Jesus Loves the Little Children, the Song and the Story. Retrieved February 3, 2014 from http://www.sharefaith.com/guide/Christian-Music/hymns-the-songs-and-the-stories/jesus-loves-the-little-children-the-song-and-the-story.html

Chapter 9

Slavery

About a year and a half ago, I met a young Vietnamese woman whose name is Nhu (pronounced *New*). Nhu grew up in Vietnam. She lived in a small village with her brothers, sisters, and her grandmother. Nhu's family was extremely poor and as a little girl she didn't have a lot of opportunity. Like most of the kids in her village, life consisted of working around the house and trying to find a way to get enough money to buy food, because in her village, food was a luxury.

When Nhu was 7 years old, she got the opportunity to attend a school that was located in a Vietnamese church. Nhu's teacher immediately began to teach her how to read and study the Bible and in just a short time, Nhu gave her life to Christ. Nhu's happiest times were being at school and serving at her church. Every Sunday, before church started, Nhu would sweep the floors and help clean the worship center before the other worshippers arrived. She loved being a part of this little congregation.

When Nhu was 12 years old, her family began to really struggle financially. They could not find work anywhere, so her grandmother borrowed money from a loan shark in order to buy food for the family. Nhu's grandmother had to pay extremely high interest on the money that she borrowed and the interest was compounded daily. To make matters worse, her grandmother didn't have a way to pay the money back.

One day, as Nhu was coming home from school, she saw her grandmother talking with a lady. This was not a normal lady. This woman was a sex broker. Sex brokers would come to Nhu's village on a consistent basis to persuade destitute families to sell their children for sex in exchange for money to pay bills and buy food. Sex brokers prey on the poor because they know that most poverty stricken people can't afford to buy the basic necessities of life for their families.

After Nhu came home from school that day, her grandmother told her that she might have to stop going to school for a while. When Nhu heard those words, she knew that her grandmother was thinking about selling her. Nhu did the only thing a 12-year-old girl could do….she prayed. She told

God that she was very scared and that she didn't want to be sold.

Three days later, the sex broker came to the village, picked Nhu up and took her to a doctor. She was taken to the physician to make sure that she was a virgin. After the doctor verified that Nhu was sexually pure, the sex broker took her to a man at a hotel. Nhu was 12 years old.

As Nhu walked into the hotel room, she was petrified. Her frail little body was shaking with fear. Nhu fell on her knees and begged the man not to hurt her. She even cried out to God for help, but her prayers went unanswered. Nhu had nowhere to go and no one who would listen. She knew that she had to do everything this man told her to do.

The next 72 hours of her life were nothing less than horrifying. For three entire days and nights, Nhu was raped, sodomized, tortured, and forced to do things that no little girl should ever have to do. She was not only robbed of her innocence, she was robbed of everything she held dear. Nhu was treated with such contempt that her perpetrator didn't even bother to give her anything to eat or drink - for three entire days!

When Nhu's "contract" was up, the sex broker came to the hotel, picked her up, and drove her back to her house. She was given some aspirin for her soreness, but she was never taken to the doctor. Nhu was in pain for two entire weeks and her heart was broken.

After her appalling experience, Nhu felt like all hope was lost. She didn't want to eat or talk to anyone. The smile that had once brightened her little Vietnamese church was gone. At night she would cry and ask God, "Why did you make me go through this? Why did you break my heart? If I didn't know you I would understand, but I know you and I loved you. God please let me be the last girl that this happens to."

Over the next six months, Nhu was sold two more times. Each time, the outcome was the same. The same abuse. The same torture. The same shame. Nhu became even more frightened, because each time she was sold, it was easier on her grandmother. Nhu was afraid that her grandmother might sell her to a brothel so that she could receive a steady income instead of just an occasional one.

After Nhu was sold the third time, she quit school. It wasn't because of her grades or even her emotional stability. Nhu quit because she found out that some of her "friends" at school had been talking about her. They told the other students that Nhu had been sold. Her life was shattered.

As I sat across the table listening to Nhu tell me her story, I was more than heartbroken. The worst part is that Nhu's story isn't an isolated case. Her story is told by millions of children all across the world.

According to UNICEF, there are 1.2 million children who are sold as sex slaves every year.[1] To put that into perspective that would be like the entire population of Dallas, Texas being sold as slaves...every year! There are more children sold as sex slaves annually than there are residents in the cities of San Jose, Indianapolis, Fort Worth, Charlotte, Cleveland, Memphis, Boston, Seattle or Denver. Staggering? You bet it is! But that is the plight of so many of the children that Jesus says he loves.

Sex slavery happens in almost every country in the world, including the United States. The Federal Bureau of Investigation has found that human sex trafficking is the most common form of modern-day slavery in America.[2] As a matter of fact, studies show that Super Bowl Sunday is one of the highest child sex trafficking days of the year in the U.S. In 2014, there were 16 children who were rescued from a forced prostitution ring during the Super Bowl festivities in and around New Jersey.[3]

Thankfully, child trafficking is illegal in the United States and there are organizations like the

FBI who are trying to prevent these kinds of events from occurring. However in other countries, there are no laws against child trafficking. Take Brazil, for example. Brazil is a country where child trafficking is not only legal; it's a form of revenue for that nation. Kathy Redmond reported that Brazil is so engrossed in the child sex trade that they have topped Thailand as the number one nation in the world for child sex trafficking. Redmond wrote:

> ...UNICEF estimates that at least 250,000 children are currently forced into prostitution in Brazil, mostly in the northeastern part of the country.
>
> "Sex tourism" in Brazil is a lucrative, booming economic industry. Organized sex tourism companies market tours for European and American men. Taxi drivers, hotel workers, and pimps work together to organize meetings between adult predators and the boys and girls. Pimps get children high on crack, then offer the children's tiny bodies to the men for a few dollars.[4]

Child sex trafficking is such a lucrative business that it has an estimated annual revenue of $32 billion, or about $87 million a day. Law enforcement authorities, government agencies, and others say human trafficking is tied with arms dealing as the world's second-largest criminal enterprise.⁵ With such huge sums of money to be made, sex brokers from all over the world swarm to impoverished cities looking for children to buy, rent, and in some cases, even steal. The children who are sold or abducted are forced to live in a state of constant fear, abuse, and torture.

One human trafficking expert told me that several years ago it would be common to find girls as young as 12 who are forced to work as sex slaves, but now there are children as young as 3 who are being sold. That wasn't a misprint. There are children as young as 3 years old who are being sold as sex slaves. Their lives consist of "working" 24 hours a day, 7 days a week, 365 days a year. Little girls (and boys) are forced to engage in sexual activity 20 to 30 times a day and if they don't thank the customer for raping them, they receive the worst beatings that you could imagine.

How Can This Happen?

When you hear of the horrendous situations that many of these children have to endure, there is a part of us that wonders, "How in the world can this happen?" The answer is found in one word. Poverty. Poverty isn't about having enough money and it's not about having enough to eat. Poverty is one of Satan's greatest tools because it rips every shred of hope out of your body cavity and leaves its victims in a state of utter hopelessness.[6]

Many Americans who hear about people living in poverty think, "Why don't those poor people just get a job? They need to get with it. They need to pull themselves up by their bootstraps and get to work."[7] From an American perspective, poor people just need a pep talk. They need a motivational message that would change their destiny,[8] but that is not the reality. If any one of us were stripped of our heritage, our can-do spirit, our education, our money and our justice system, we would come to the conclusion that we don't know what to do because I can't read.[9] I've never been to school. I have no money. No place to live. No shoes. No clothes. No food. I have absolutely nothing. That is the heart and soul of true poverty.[10]

And can I tell you something? There are children all over the world who live in that kind of poverty every single day. If you are a poverty-stricken child, the forecast for your life is extremely dim. What often happens in many third world countries is when parents are struggling financially, when they can't feed their children, parents often do things that they wouldn't normally do. The most common thing is to sell one of their children into some type of slavery to ease their financial pressure.

The Antidote

If this is the first time you are learning about human trafficking, it may be difficult to digest. But you need to know there is a solution. There is an antidote that can alleviate the suffering and pain that so many of these children face. The answer is found in sponsorship. When you sponsor a child of poverty, you not only rescue them from sex brokers and predators, you are changing the course of that child's life.

While I can't give you an exhaustive list of organizations that rescue children of poverty through sponsorship, I can give you two that I highly recommend. I have worked with these two organizations over the years and they are, hands down, the best on the planet when it comes to rescuing children who live in poverty.

Remember Nhu

Remember Nhu was started back in 2005 by Carl and Laura Ralston. Carl was a hot shot, super successful, entrepreneur in the insurance world. He had everything you could imagine. He had the house, the car, the wardrobe, and the financial freedom. In the eyes of the world, he had it all. However, with all his money and status, Carl wasn't content.

In 2005, Carl went to a seminar and God completely wrecked his heart - in a good way. As Carl was sitting in this sea of people, a man began talking about a little girl named Nhu, yes the very same girl whose story I told you at the beginning of the chapter. When Carl heard Nhu's story, his heart literally broke. As he was sitting in this huge auditorium filled with people, the Holy Spirit spoke two words to him, "Remember Nhu."

Carl went home and told his wife Laura that he had to do something to stop little girls from being sold as sex slaves. A short time later, Carl sold his insurance company and started a non-profit organization called Remember Nhu (remembernhu.org) to eradicate the use of children in the sex trade industry. Carl has spent the past nine years establishing homes all over the world for young girls to live, so they can avoid being sold into the sex trade.

Each sponsored child lives in a safe home with house parents. She is given an education, food, shelter, health care, and is taught about God's love on a consistent basis. Each little girl is sponsored all the way through college so that there is no chance of them falling prey to a sex broker.

Compassion International

Compassion International was started in 1952 by a pastor whose name was Everett Swanson. He was on a preaching tour in South Korea when he encountered the bitter poverty of Korea's unwanted children. After he saw the brutal conditions they were living in, Swanson knew he had to do something about it.

When Swanson came back to the United States, he established a program that allowed caring people to provide food, shelter, education, medical care, and Christian training for Korean orphans. That program was and remains the emphasis of Compassion International.

Today Compassion serves over 1.3 million children in 26 different countries and they are dedicated to releasing children from poverty by providing programs that enable children to grow up without being hungry and without the fear of being sold into slavery. Each sponsored child receives regular Christian training, healthcare, hygiene training, food, and a safe Christian environment to grow in God's love.

How Sponsorship Works

The way that both Remember Nhu and Compassion International work is they ask an individual or a family to sponsor a child from any country that they choose. Each sponsor pays a monthly amount that ranges from $38 (Compassion) to $50 (Remember Nhu) a month. That money does not go for a bunch of administration costs and fees. Those resources go directly to putting a child in a safe environment, it gives them an education, and it keeps young people, both boys and girls, out of slavery.

You Can Make A Difference

If you live in the United States of America, you are among the world's wealthiest people. According to a recent Gallop pole, the average worker in America earns $43,585 a year.[11] Even if you work a minimum wage job, by the world's standards, you are exceedingly rich because studies show that almost half of the world - over three billion people - live on less than $2.50 a day.[12]

Since we as a nation have been blessed so much financially, wouldn't it make sense for us (and our churches) to start sponsoring hundreds and thousands of children in poverty? Wouldn't it make sense to make children matter around the world by taking some of the monetary riches that God has given us and distribute that wealth to our brothers and sisters in Christ? Isn't the Bible totally clear on this issue? Isn't that why I John 3:17 says:

> If anyone has material possessions and sees a brother or sister in need but has no pity on them, how can the love of God be in that person?

You don't need to be a theologian to break down that verse. It's really simple.

- If anyone has material possessions – that's us!
- And sees a brother or sister in need – that's the children of poverty.
- But has no pity on them – that means if we don't take action and do something like sponsorship.
- How could the love of God be in that person? The answer is….it can't.

You see, it's one thing to get emotional when you hear a story like Nhu's. It's another thing to get angry when you hear of how many children are sold into slavery, but the issue of ending child slavery is going to take more than emotion. It's going to take people like you to actually get involved to alleviate the problem by sponsoring a child.

Did you ever wonder what would happen if every follower of Jesus in America would sponsor a child of poverty? What would happen if every pastor in America challenged the people in his or her congregation to sponsor a child? The result would be the end of poverty and the end of child slavery. You can make children matter all over the world by sponsoring a child. All you have to do is go to their websites Compassion.com or Remembernhu.org and follow the links. If you want to make children matter around the world, the easiest way to do that is through sponsorship.

1. Dottridge, M. (2006). Reference Guide On Protecting the Rights of Child Victims of Trafficking In Europe. Retrieved February 4, 2014, from http://www.unicef.org/ceecis/UNICEF_Child_Trafficking14-43.pdf

2. Rodriguez, A. and Hill, R. (2011, March). Human Sex Trafickling. Retrieved February 5, 2014, from http://www.fbi.gov/stats-services/publications/law-enforcement-bulletin/march_2011/human_sex_trafficking

3. Winter, M. (2014, February 4). FBI: Kids 13 to 17 rescued from Super Bowl prostitution. USA TODAY. Retrieved February 4, 2014, from http://www.usatoday.com/story/news/nation/2014/02/04/super-bowl-prostitution/5207399/

4. Redmond, K. (2012). Called Into the Trenches. Retrieved February 5, 2014, from http://www.compassion.com/magazine/prevent-child-abuse.htm

5. Neubauer, C. (2011, April 23). Sex trafficking in the U.S. called 'epidemic'. Washington Times. Retrieved February 5, 2014, from http://www.washingtontimes.com/news/2011/apr/23/sex-trafficking-us-called-epidemic/?page=all

6. Stafford, W. (2007). Too Small To Ignore: Why the Least of These Matters Most. Colorado Springs, CO: Waterbrook Press.

7. Stafford, W. (2007). Too Small To Ignore: Why the Least of These Matters Most. Colorado Springs, CO: Waterbrook Press.

8. Stafford, W. (2007). Too Small To Ignore: Why the Least of These Matters Most. Colorado Springs, CO: Waterbrook Press.

9. Stafford, W. (2007). Too Small To Ignore: Why the Least of These Matters Most. Colorado Springs, CO: Waterbrook Press.

10. Stafford, W. (2007). Too Small To Ignore: Why the Least of These Matters Most. Colorado Springs, CO: Waterbrook Press.

11. Shah, A. (2013, January 7). Poverty Facts and Stats. Global Issues. Retrieved February 5, 2014, from http://www.globalissues.org/article/26/poverty-facts-and-stats

12. Phelps, G. and Crabtree, S. (2013, December 16). Worldwide, Median Income About $10,000. Gallop World. Retrieved February 5, 2014, from http://www.gallup.com/poll/166211/worldwide-median-household-income-000.aspx

Conclusion

As I thought about how I wanted to end this book, there were several different things that came to mind. I thought about listing all the possible things someone could do to make children matter in their home, church, city, or even around the world. I considered giving you an action plan of different steps you could follow in each area. However, the more I thought about it, I decided to go in a different direction. What I would like to do is leave you with two questions.

The first question is this: What has Jesus been saying to you as you've read this book? Have the words of Jesus been speaking to your heart about your own children? Has the Holy Spirit challenged you to be more proactive in discipling your son or daughter? Is Jesus telling you to find a child or teenager in your church whose home life is completely wrecked and to pour your life and love into them? Are you more excited than you've ever been about giving students opportunities to serve at your church on a consistent basis? Are you more committed than ever to be a congregation that impacts the children in your city by volunteering, throwing parties, and partnering with your school system? What has Jesus been saying to you?

Has he been telling you that children really are the most important people in the world? Is it clear that children are priceless and they should never be sold into slavery? Has the Holy Spirit challenged you to sponsor a child of poverty? Has Jesus been telling you to sacrifice some of your time, your money, and even your church budget to make an impact in the life of a child? What has Jesus been saying to you?

The second question I want to leave you with is this: What are you going to do about it? If Jesus has been speaking something to your heart, what are you going to do about it? Are you going to ignore it? Are you going to push the words of Jesus to the back of your mind and simply return to life-as-usual, or are you actually going to do something to make children matter?

I'm going to ask that you would never forget what Jesus has been saying to you about children and I would almost beg you to do something about it. There are children all over the world whose lives would forever be changed if the followers of Jesus would take his words about children seriously, because even the smallest act of kindness can make the biggest difference.

Years ago, a freelance reporter from the *New York Times* was interviewing Marilyn Monroe. The reporter was aware that during her childhood years Marilyn Monroe had been shuffled from one foster home to another, so this reporter asked her, "Marilyn, did you ever feel loved by any of the foster families that you lived with?"

Monroe thought for a moment and then said, "Once. When I was about seven or eight years old, the woman I was living with was putting on makeup and I was watching her. She was in a really good mood that night, so she reached over and patted my cheeks with her rouge puff and for that moment I felt loved by her."

The reporter wrote, "As Marilyn Monroe told of this event, tears were streaming down her face. Why? The touch lasted only brief moment. It happened years ago. It was done in a casual, playful way, not in an attempt to communicate great warmth or meaning. But as small of an act as it was, it was like pouring buckets of love on the life of a little girl starved for affection."[1]

There are children just like that all over the world. You (personally) and your church (holistically) can make a difference in their life. We just need to take our cue from Jesus and do everything we can to truly make children matter.

---

1. Colton, H. (1983). The Gift of Touch. New York: Seaview/Putnam